Supporting Indigenous Ministries

With Selected Readings

D0166573

A ♦ B G C ♦ MONOGRAPH

With Thanks to the Contributors

PANYA BABA
President, Evangelical Church of West Africa

JOHN C. BENNETT
President, Overseas Council for Theological Education and Missions

DAVID J. BOSCH
Late editor of *Missionalia* and Head of Missiology at the University of South Africa

LUIS BUSH
International Director, A. D. 2000 and Beyond

DAVID HOWARD
President, Latin America Mission

LAUSANNE OCCASIONAL PAPERS
Lausanne Committee for World Evangelization

GEORGE W. PETERS
Late Professor of Missions at Dallas Theological Seminary

DANIEL RICKETT
Director of Salt and Light for Partners International

JOHN SIEWERT
Editor of *Mission Handbook,* MARC/World Vision Int.

CHARLES R. TABER
Professor of World Mission, Emmanuel School of Religion

WILLIAM TAYLOR
Executive Director, Missions Commission, World Evangelical Fellowship

Supporting Indigenous Ministries

With Selected Readings

Edited by

Daniel Rickett and Dotsey Welliver

BILLY GRAHAM CENTER
Wheaton College · Wheaton, Illinois 60187-5593

Published by the Billy Graham Center
Wheaton College
Wheaton, IL 60187-5593

Printed in the United States of America

ISBN 879089-26-2

For information about other publications or the resources of the Billy Graham Center, E-mail BGCADM@wheaton.edu or visit our web site: http://www.wheaton.edu.

Contents

Foreword

Charles Van Engen[1]

We are at the threshold of the most significant era of world Christian mission ever in the history of the Church. Two-thirds of all Christians today live in Africa, Asia, Latin America, and Oceania. Just as the Christian church's origins were Middle-Eastern and North African, so today the church is again made up predominantly of Christians in the Two-Thirds World.

As Gordon Aeschliman has reminded us, "Spanish is the language most spoken by Christians around the world; English is second. In 1800, 86 percent of all Christians were White; by the year 2000 that proportion will have dropped to 39 percent. The world's largest congregation is in Korea; the biggest church building in Côte D'Ivoire (formerly Ivory Coast). From a purely statistical point of view, Christianity is a non-Western religion. This reality has yet to impact the majority of us in the United States, but we will experience it in the final decade of the twentieth century."[2]

Although more than four billion people still do not know Jesus Christ as Savior and Lord, around one-and-a-half billion people now consider themselves Christian, circling the globe. In spite of the obvious needs facing the church, Christians around the world today speak more languages, possess greater resources, have the Bible available in more languages, have greater facility of travel and communication, have more qualified leaders, have a deeper awareness of the cultural imprisonment of the Gospel, and possess a deeper sensitivity to the cultural issues in mission than at any time in the church's history. We are not at the sunset of Christian mission, but rather at the sunrise of the most exciting and extensive era ever in its history.

The reality now facing the church calls for all of us, using Paul Hiebert's phrase, to make a radical shift "beyond anti-colonialism to globalism"[3] in our missiological thought and action. Such a new reality highlights the timeliness, urgency, and significance of the first Consultation on Support of Indigenous Ministries, out of which this book has come. This conference was important on at least four fronts.

First, the presentations, papers, and resources documented in this volume represent a surprisingly large number of agencies who consider themselves involved in "support of indigenous ministries." The very helpful "Directory of Organizations" included in the book witnesses to the breadth of involvement in this topic on the part of North American mission-sending agencies.

Second, the tone from the conference is not one of triumphalism, trying to fix something broken, having all the answers, promoting certain agencies, or rehashing old agendas. Rather, there is a beginning move toward self-examination, rethinking old habits and patterns, and creating openness to new ways of addressing very complex and historically entrenched patterns of mission behavior.[4]

Third, coursing through all the presentations is an evident desire to find new ways to move beyond dependency through independence to true interdependence in mature partnerships for world evangelization. As Charles Taber and a number of others emphasize, here is a search for means whereby the Body of Christ on a global scale may cooperate and partner as one Body together, in true mutuality (David Bosch's term) for world evangelization.

Fourth, this consultation represents an attempt to bridge between mission arenas that have been operating too disconnected from each other: missiological reflection and mission administration; Western mission-sending with mission-sending from Asia, Africa, and Latin America; and sending churches and agencies in relationship to receiving churches and agencies on a global scale.

This volume is being prepared in time for the second consultation, scheduled for September, 1997. Here the reader can plunge into the headwaters of what many of us hope will become the rushing stream of a new movement in global mission partnerships: bilateral and multilateral, bicultural and multicultural. The urgency of just such a movement can be appreciated by a glance at the list of titles of articles and books that have been included in the "Selected Readings." Although church and mission have radically globalized, especially during the 1990s, is it not odd that in the selections offered there are only three books and five articles directly related to the topic of the consultation? This vacuum does not represent an oversight on the part of the editors. Other missiologists and I have been watching the literature over the last several years for related books and articles and have found mission publications sadly silent on the issue. Thus the importance of this volume.

The reader will also find sprinkled throughout the book a number of helpful suggestions, processes, and perspectives that it would behoove Christian churches and mission everywhere to put increasingly into practice. This book needs to be read by local church pastors and mission committees, cross-cultural missionaries (no matter what their country of origin might be), and mission executives all over the world, as well as supporters and personnel of sending and receiving churches and mission agencies. For many readers, the second section of "Selected Readings" will provide very constructive background to rethinking patterns of paternalism in mission that have plagued us for so long.

Having been personally involved in emotional and stressful negotiations between my sending church and mission and the National Presbyterian Church of Mexico during and immediately following the days of "moratorium" that colored much of our discussions in the early 1970s, I was fascinated, stimulated, and helped by reading this book.

This volume reminds us that paternalism is an ever-present danger in mission and ministry. And paternalism is not simply a matter of money. It goes far broader and deeper than material resources. At bottom, it is a relational and faith issue impacted by the perceptions of the participants of their discipleship and mutuality before Christ in God's world. Shades of paternalism appear mostly when we hold to some position or idea in a doctrinaire fashion, or take some action regardless of the circumstances, opinions, wisdom, or feelings of the people we are called to serve—with whom we serve. It is not a respecter of cultures and will rear its ugly head as much among Two-Thirds World mission-sending agencies as among Western ones. Probably none of us can escape paternalism altogether. Yet the dangers of paternalism should not deter us from finding ways in which to share globally the church's resources for world mission—especially in terms of supporting indigenous ministries.

As several authors point out, personal relationships are absolutely key for addressing issues of paternalism. Maybe all we can do is be aware of these traps—and learn from each other (both those who send and those who receive). In each decision, each circumstance, at the initiation of each new program, in the training of each new person for cross-cultural mission, we need to pray much for wisdom, sensitivity, and self-giving love—and then ceaselessly evaluate our thinking, values, and behavior in relation to those traps.

Ultimately we need to be aware that globally, there is one Spirit, one Body, one hope and calling. Together, as multicultural members of one Church, seeking to work together as mutual partners, together we seek to be Christ's Church in a particular place and specific culture.

There need be no "us-and-them" mentality—and there cannot be. All of us together must seek to be obedient to one Lord who is present in each and every place. Donors and recipients together need to share their visions, goals, and strategies, and work as adults, equals, mutual disciples of Jesus, actively cooperative, and mutually-accountable partners. Then many of the pitfalls of paternalism may be avoided, and healthy, loving, visionary, and creative mission may be undertaken.

May our loving Lord Jesus Christ, in whose mission we participate, guide us all as world Christians to explore new ways to partner together in the evangelization (wholistic, incarnational, and transformational) of the more than four billion who yet do not know Jesus Christ.

Endnotes

1. Charles (Chuck) Van Engen was born and raised in Mexico of missionary parents. From 1973 to 1985 he was a missionary of the Reformed Church in America, serving in partnership with the National Presbyterian Church of Mexico in theological education, evangelism, youth ministries, camping ministries, and refugee relief. He is presently Arthur F. Glasser Professor of Biblical Theology of Mission at Fuller Theological Seminary's School of World Mission in Pasadena, California.

2. Gordon Aeschliman, *Global Trends: Ten Changes Affecting Christians Everywhere* (Downers Grove: InterVarsity Press, 1990), 109.

3. Paul Hiebert, "Beyond Anti-Colonialism to Globalism," *Missiology* XIX, no. 2 (July 1991): 263–282.

4. I say this, even though I am not enthusiastic about the word "indigenous" in the title of the conference and the book, given its substantial baggage in Christian mission—much of which was in fact rather heavily paternalistic. Whether there is any better word to use is open to question.

Preface

This book is a response to a historical moment. It chronicles the inaugural Consultation on Support of Indigenous Ministries. Until recently, few mission agencies in the Western world existed specifically to assist and enhance the work of indigenous ministries. In the past decade, however, partnership with independent ministries of the non-Western world has become widely accepted. A score of new agencies has emerged for that specific purpose. Some traditional Western mission sending agencies are now also adding separate programs to support indigenous ministries.

When first planning the consultation, it was estimated some 30 agencies might attend. After an initial survey, more than 113 U. S. mission agencies identified themselves as being primarily concerned with supporting independent missionary movements in the non-Western world.

Sensing the time was right for such agencies to meet, Chuck Bennett of Partners International conferred with Jim Kraakevik, at that time director of the Billy Graham Center in Wheaton, and Bernie May, head of a new division for indigenous translators at Wycliffe Bible Translators. A planning committee was formed, consisting of John Bennett (Overseas Council), Bernie May (The Seed Company, Wycliffe), Chuck Bennett (Partners International), Ken Gill (Billy Graham Center), Lewis Abbott (Ambassadors for Christ International), and Daniel Rickett (Salt and Light).

The purpose was to convene a consultation of U. S. agencies whose primary concern is supporting indigenous ministries. The consultation was designed to accomplish the following basic objectives.

- Get to know other people and agencies engaged in similar ministries
- Learn how to make our ministries more effective
- Identify key trends and specific strategies for the future
- Discover how to motivate more Christians in America to support indigenous work.

More than 100 representatives of 52 agencies assembled at the Billy Graham Center, Wheaton, Illinois from October 17–20, 1996. The program consisted of morning devotionals followed by plenary sessions on trends and critical issues. Discussions continued in specialized workshops, periodic reality checks throughout the consultation, and working groups. The presentations, discussions, and working group issues form the basis of this book.

One evening was given to honoring the pioneers of the movement. Presentations were made to Allen Finley of Partners International, Bob Finley of Christian Aid Mission, and Ian North of Ambassadors for Christ International. A special musical concert by John G. Elliott closed the evening in a memorable time of worship.

By the last day, working groups brought together proposals to form an ongoing fellowship, to meet again in 1997, and to begin an Internet cyberspace conference on issues regarding indigenous missions. Those issues include:

(1) accountability by indigenous missionaries
(2) church and denominational relations
(3) dependency and interdependency with overseas partners
(4) fundraising
(5) future planning
(6) linkages with traditional mission agencies
(7) mutual accountability
(8) standards of practice
(9) vision sharing with the whole Church

The consultation concluded with a time of worship, acknowledging our oneness in Christ by sharing in holy communion. It was a solemn and precious moment, especially as we considered the great body of God's servants whom we seek to enable and support in the ministry of the Gospel.

Overview of Contents

In Section One, Panya Baba, whose address concluded the consultation, represents not only the end of our efforts, but the future of world evangelization. Baba speaks personally to three defining factors of cooperation in the Gospel: our common ground of brotherhood in Christ, our common cause of world evangelization, and our differences in gifts and abilities which make partnership not only possible but necessary. Luis Bush outlines eight trends related to the support of indigenous ministries, and cautions the movement from becoming conventional rather than radical, transactional rather than transformational, and rational rather than relational. William Taylor takes issue with parochial views that set native missionaries against foreign missionaries, West against non-West, church against mission, and offers several suggestions for building community, beginning with "discovering a sense of the Body of Christ." David Howard defines the crux of the dependency/interdependency question as an issue of responsibility, illustrating from the history of the Latin America Mission. Finally, John Bennett sums up by condensing the many discussions and results of the working groups of the consultation.

Section Two includes three indispensable articles on partnership in mission by distinguished missiologists David J. Bosch, George W. Peters, and Charles R. Taber, and a selection from *Co-operating in World Evangelization* by the Lausanne Committee for World Evangelization.

Section Three is a directory of organizations which support indigenous ministries. A summary of findings and brief profiles on each ministry are included.

The appendices include survey results of "best reading" on the subject; and a selected list of books and articles for further reading.

It is hoped that this book will stimulate further discussion and contribute to the growing awareness that missionaries of other nations deserve the same love and support we afford our own sons and daughters.

Daniel Rickett

Acknowledgments

Our thanks go to the following for permission to reprint the articles in Section 2, Selected Readings:

David J. Bosch. "Towards True Mutuality: Exchanging the Same Commodities or Supplementing Each Others' Needs?" *Missiology: An International Review* 6 (3): July 1978. Reprinted by permission of Mrs. Annemie Bosch and *Missiology.* All rights reserved.

Lausanne Committee for World Evangelization. "Hindrances to Cooperation: The Suspicion about Finances." Reprinted by permission of Lausanne Committee for World Evangelization from the book, *Co-Operating in World Evangelization,* Lausanne Occasional Papers 24, 1983. All rights reserved.

George W. Peters. "Pauline Patterns of Church-Mission Relationships." *Evangelical Missions Quarterly* 9: Winter 1973. Reprinted by permission of *Evangelical Missions Quarterly.* All rights reserved.

Charles R. Taber. "Structures and Strategies for Interdependence in World Mission." Reprinted by permission of Herald Press, Scottdale, PA 15683 from the book, *Mission Focus: Current Issues,* Wilbert R. Shenk, Editor, 1980. All rights reserved.

Special thanks to Marty Barclay for her transcription and word processing of the original talks given at the consultation. Lynda Johnson and Gerry Barnes provided significant help in the task of editing consultation papers.

We also express our thanks to John Siewert and MARC/World Vision for their help in providing the Directory of Organizations in Section 3.

CHAPTER 1

Facing Disturbing Issues
The Ground of Cooperation in the Gospel

Panya Baba

I would like to give a special thanks to Partners International because of their contribution and partnership with us in the work of evangelism and church planting in Nigeria and to six other African countries where our missionaries are working. We give glory to God for the concern and encouragement that we have been receiving. I come from a very mission-minded church that has about 3000 local congregations in Nigeria alone. We thank God for what He is doing through our church.

We started in 1949 by sending two missionary couples. Through the teaching of the Word of God, we understood we are part and parcel of the universal Church of Christ—the Body of Christ. We began to understand that we are responsible for the global missionary work beginning in our own country. We are responsible to share the gospel with our fellow Africans as well. So we started by sending two missionaries. Now this mission has grown up, and we have 1200 cross-cultural missionaries in Africa.

We thank God because missions has gone deep into the heart of our churches. Last year our total budget was about $2.4 million. We received some 20 percent of this from Western countries. There are pastors who openly tell their congregations, "Until I see most of our offerings going for mission—for seeking the lost—I will not be satisfied." The Lord is doing wonderful things. But I would like to challenge you.

"For there is no difference between Jew and Gentile—the same Lord is Lord of all and richly blesses all who call on him, for, 'Everyone who calls on the name of the Lord will be saved.' How, then, can they call on the one they have not believed in? And how can they believe in the one of whom they have not heard? And how can they hear without someone preaching to them? And how can they preach unless they are sent? As it is written, 'How beautiful are the feet of those who bring good news!'" (Romans 10:12–15).

I have found that partnership is not only needed, especially as we face the finishing task of world evangelization in our generation, but it is a necessity—the necessity of partnership. We have no choice. What are the steps to be taken so that we will be penetrating more among the greatest unreached people groups, one of which is the Muslims, both in our own country and especially in the North African countries—and if possible into the Middle East?

In one consultation I asked key leaders to come and share with us. I still remember the testimony given to us by a minister from Iran. He said, "I have a very heavy burden and heavy heart because our people have never given sufficient time—enough time—to know God loves them in Jesus Christ. They have never given enough time to hear the gospel and say *yes* to Christ, or even *no* to Christ. They have not yet given enough time." As he said that, he burst into tears.

He went back to Iran, and several months later I received information that he had been kidnapped and was found murdered. His words are still ringing in my heart…in my mind. "Our people have never given enough time to say either *yes* or *no*." He was in tears because he knew his people must pay a price just to accept the free gift of salvation and forgiveness as all of us have.

As I see what the Holy Spirit is doing, I realize that unless partnership is done—which is to me a necessity, we have no choice—it may still take another 2000 years before we finish our assignment of global evangelization.

The passage in Romans is very disturbing. Partnership is a necessity because of these disturbing issues in the Bible—disturbing words, disturbing voices, disturbing questions—that are still relevant in our generation concerning world evangelization. They are disturbing not only to the Apostle Paul, but to God himself. In Ezekiel 33:11, God testified that He came to open his wound in his heart so we can speak to Him as a human being. He said, "As long as I live, I have no pleasure in the death of the wicked." It is very disturbing to Him since He testified this to one of his prophets…tell them…tell the chosen people. And I believe He says, "Tell them in the West. Tell them in Africa. Tell them in Asia. Tell them in Latin America. As long as I live I have no pleasure at all in the death of the wicked."

I ask myself, "Is this how his heart is?" Actually, I take Ezekiel 33:11 as a spiritual x-ray of the heart of God, so that we can test it. We can see clearly his heartbeat. So when He has no pleasure for one, how much concern, how much burden, how much heaviness does He have for millions of sinners? I ask myself, "Why? Why? Why even for one wicked person?" Because in every person—every living human being—there is part and parcel of God himself in that human being whether he or she is white, black, yellow, or red. When the sinner dies and goes to hell, it pains Him because part and parcel of Himself is being destroyed—is going to everlasting punishment. So it's very disturbing to Him.

The Bible says God so loved the world that He gave his only begotten son. When He demonstrated this, He was not just talking hyperbole to excite them. He demonstrated—He put it into action—so that we should know that He gave all the best He had. He gave his only begotten Son for the whole world. Our God is a global missionary God. Who can say the Church is responsible for evangelism in their local area alone or in their country alone? Who will say this when He himself— the Messiah—is indeed the global missionary God.

The Bible does not say He loved a section of the world—the Western countries. Africa is included. You want to follow the love of God? You must pray for Africa. You must be concerned about Africa. And you must pray for Asia. Latin America too. The whole world, God says. Go into the whole world and preach the gospel to every creature. Everything is global because the whole world, if it perishes, disturbs Jesus.

Matthew recorded his observation and his testimony in chapter 9. He said, *Jesus went about all towns and villages.* Why? Disturbing. And as He went farther out, when He saw the crowd He had compassion. Not only that, he shared with his followers, *the harvest is plenteous but the workers are few.* That was a cry from Christ. He asked them to participate, to cooperate and join him. There is not a single church in the world that has no role to play. Let's keep this in mind as we explore partnership. What about the churches in Two-Thirds World countries? The church, wherever it is, is responsible for the gospel within and without. Because our God is a global missionary God.

Would you pray that the Lord of the harvest will send the workers into the harvest? How can they call without believing? How can they believe without hearing? How can they hear without a preacher? How can they preach unless they are sent? There must be some who will go, and there must be senders. This is God's plan. This is an invitation for churches in the West to be the senders—to be the supporters—and pray because we are entering the new era of mission.

The traffic is no more one way. The assignment is too gigantic. Two thousand years are about to come to an end. The Holy Spirit Himself— the Lord of the harvest Himself—now is moving. He is raising helping hands from Western churches and Western missions because of the serious condition that Jesus gave in Matthew 24:14, that this gospel of the kingdom will be preached in the whole world. Then the end will come. Are we fully aware that the whole world is waiting for that greatest one event?

Jesus' Second Coming will happen. Who can sleep on this? I am having sleepless nights about our people. They have not been given enough. It is not only our people. There are still many unreached people groups today in many countries. This is very disturbing to Jesus. And it was disturbing to the Apostle Paul, to the point that he had to change his life priority. He said when he was called as a missionary, all the things that were gained, he had to renounce and count them loss. Why? Because Christ had delegated this wonderful ministry to him.

Later on we find Paul saying, "I press on." It's not the voice of a tired, retired person in a satisfactory kind of ministry. It's an ambitious voice—a military voice—from somebody who had gone out. May the Lord help us. At the end he told his fellow missionaries in Philippi, he told the local church pastor, "Why? Why are you crying for me? So do you want to discourage me? You want to make me frustrated to fulfill the will of God? I am ready, not only to suffer, but to die." What a total commitment—one we need to learn. Global ministry must be accomplished by global cooperation and global partnership.

I want to congratulate Partners International and some of the other organizations that have taken a bold step for this kind of partnership. Why? You know, partnership didn't begin in the twentieth century. It didn't begin in the nineteenth century. It didn't begin in the eighteenth century. It began in the first century, during the first launching of the cross-cultural missionary global world mission. We know. We have the documents. To the local church at Philippi, Paul was an indigenous pastor in Asia. Back in Macedonia the church took seriously the support of that missionary. Paul said, "I thank you for your partnership." In Philippians 2 he said, "God who started this wonderful and good work"—that is, sponsorship of the cross-cultural evangelism that initiated an era in the church of Antioch.

At the end in chapter 4, Paul said, "I thank you that you have brought back your thought towards me." He thanked them that they had come back, since there was a time when perhaps it seemed they had forgotten. "I rejoice greatly in the Lord that at last you have renewed your concern." Partnership is biblical. That's why I congratulate you, because you are bringing back the real pattern of how global world evangelization started. And I pray that God will continue to bless this effort.

How about our Body? The gospel has done very wonderful things to us all. In Ephesians, Paul called it the *mystery of the gospel* because in the gospel we join together. And our leader has stated that there is no difference between Jews and Greek. The oneness of the body, which is the mystery of the gospel, is the real definition and description of what the Holy Spirit is leading you to do. We in partnership are all different members with different functions, but we have one common goal—cooperating together so that sinners will be saved. We cannot do this without the love of Christ. But Jesus said, "Do this in remembrance of me." He did not ask us to remember one of his miracles—healing, as good as it is. He said, do this for remembrance. Remembrance of what? Remembrance of his love. Remembrance of how He gave his life for us.

Jesus demanded only love for this kind of partnership. Only oneness in him. After Peter had denied Christ, Jesus asked him three times, "Peter, do you love me?" (John 21). The only qualification he desires from you and me is love. Loving Christ. Loving each other. Paul said, "The love of Christ constrains me."

Jesus asks each of us, "Do you love me?" It goes beyond just giving money. Partnership demands more. In Nigeria it breaks my heart to see the graves of the missionaries who served there. In less than a year after arrival, some were buried in my country—in my fatherland. What constrained them? Just the love of Christ. Money was secondary. Partnership demands our lives—the sacrifice of our lives. If our life is given, what else is needed?

Every one of us has a role to play. True, the Third-World countries might not have money, but they can give themselves, their lives, their time. Peter said, "Gold and silver, we have not. But we have Jesus Christ." You have given Jesus to us. We have something to share. So we've both got to do it. Whatever we can. Whatever the Third-World countries can. Despite the poverty. Poverty cannot stop us from missions if our hearts are filled with love.

Accountability is important and necessary, but I have been discovering an accountability in the Bible that is beyond a routine or paper accountability. Our accountability is to God. When we are giving accountability to God, accountability to our brother will be easy.

The demand of the Macedonian call today is so great. Paul said to the church in Philadelphia, "I know you have little strength. The lack of strength could be financial. It could be economical. It could be education. But I have set an open door before you." Then Paul heard another voice, a disturbing one, crying out "help us!" May the Lord help all of us to do our part in bringing the lost to Christ.

CHAPTER 2

Greater Glory Yet to Come
Trends Regarding Indigenous Ministries

Luis Bush

We are all interested in trends associated with indigenous ministries. But first, a few words in pursuit of the meaning of the term *indigenous*.

The words that are noted as synonyms are filled with meaning that creates mental pictures not always that affirming. For example, terms are used like: *native, national, inborn, aboriginal, autochthonous, homegrown, inbred, inherent, natural, original, spontaneous, unacquired*. Some related words are even stronger: *barbarian, primeval, primitive, primordial, pristine, savage*. This is true even as one pursues the relating contrasted words such as *advanced, progressive, civilized, cultured*.

It becomes difficult to find a term describing indigenous that is not demeaning. However, when you look at the English usage of the associated term *native*, two British sources, Longman 1984 and Sellers 1975, note that native for a nonwhite, non-European person is no longer considered polite. The offensiveness of the word seems to be an embedded reaction to colonialism and its attitudes. The word is certainly charged with racial overtones in certain places such as South Africa. The term "national" also carries a demeaning intonation in the minds of some. Some of the exchangeable terms are rather nebulous. In Spanish, indigenous is the word used for native Indian. In the Hispanic world we would use the word *autochtonous* to most clearly describe the term indigenous as currently used in the English language.

Webster's Dictionary defines indigenous as "having originated in and being produced, growing, living, or occurring naturally in a particular region or environment." A typical usage today might be something like, "The indigenous people of Indonesia are mostly of mixed Malay stock. The most distinct ethnic groups are the Javanese and the Sundanese." We are in a consultation of Christians who seek to support ministries originating from and growing in geographic regions of the world other than our own. Thus, these distinctions and the wording used becomes more challenging every day.

My perspective is colored by a recent five weeks in different parts of India and at the triennial National Consultation on Evangelism there. These perceptions are also based on reflection of Scripture from the book of Luke.

Also a dispute arose among them as to which of them was considered to be greatest. Jesus said to them, "The kings of the Gentiles lord it over them; and those who exercise authority over them call themselves Benefactors. But you are not to be like that. Instead, the greatest among you should be like the youngest, and the one who rules like the one who serves. For who is greater, the one who is at the table or the one who serves? Is it not the one who is at the table? But I am among you as one who serves" (Luke 22:24–27).

Jesus' followers were excited about *which of them was considered to be greatest*. This is surprising in view of what Jesus had just said about one of them betraying Him. Jesus then told them that such thinking is like that of the world. His followers should each desire to be *one who serves*. For Jesus was among them as One who serves (*diakonoun*, serves in a lowly way). They were excited about being the greatest. The Lord's excitement was that they learn, like Him, to be servant of all. On this He would build his kingdom. With this in mind, let's look at the trends.

Great Expectancy with Regard to the Lord's Return

TIME magazine (October 11, 1993) reported the story of an earthquake in India with the title, "While They Slept."

With the head of an elephant and the body of a potbellied man, Lord Ganesha is one of Hinduism's most beloved deities, a god of new beginnings and good luck. Multitudes of peasants in the hinterland reaches of Maharashtra, a western Indian state that is home to the god's most devout cult...were concluding a 10-day festival in Ganesha's honor, celebrated late into the night with dancing, singing, and blowing horns. In Killari, a village of about 15,500 near the Karnataka state border, the ceremonies culminated in the ritual dipping of the god's idols in the village pond. Around 1 a.m., worshipers straggled home and fell into a deep slumber. It was a sleep from which most of them never awoke. At 3:56 a.m., an earthquake struck with a deafening roar and a rattling movement that swept across the southern sector of the Deccan Plateau.

What *TIME* did not report was that the earthquake occurred while a Christian geologist in the nearby state of Andra Pradesh was sleeping. He and his wife were awakened by the windows shaking. When he realized that it was an earthquake, he immediately began to reflect upon the subterranean geological map and soon became aware that something really strange was happening. Was that not a stable continental region?

Curious, he looked into the matter further. It might have seemed an inconsequential matter, but this was not an ordinary scientist. This was the man who had been instrumental in discovering the largest coal seam in the world and who moved the country of India from 20 percent self-sufficient to 70 percent self-sufficient in oil. He was awarded the Scientist of the Year award last year for India, perhaps the first Christian to be so honored.

His suspicion was confirmed when top geologists in India gathered to reflect upon what had happened. In their collection of written essays published in 1994 in a book titled *The Lattur Earthquake,* geologists from the Geological Society of India grappled with the puzzling location of the earthquake. The editor concluded with the remarks, "The quake will go down in history as the deadliest earthquake to strike a stable continental region. The quake occurred in a region that has long since been considered immune to such shock."

That October following the earthquake, the Christian scientist, Professor B. E. Vijayam (affectionately called Viji), found an explanation of the phenomena that satisfied his scientific, Christian mindset. The timing coincided with Day One of the global prayer initiative focused on the 10/40 Window, "Praying Through the Window I," taking place in October, 1993. On that October 1, seventeen million Christians around the world focused their prayer on the country that appeared first on their prayer calendar. That country was India.

Viji found the answer to the mystery of the great shock in a "so-called" shock-immune region. When our Lord responded to the question of the disciples, "What shall be the sign of thy coming, and of the end of the world," among other things He said, "...there shall be...earthquakes in diverse places." This triggered something in the heart of Viji that crystallized as he read further in Matthew. "And this gospel of the kingdom will be preached in the whole world as a testimony to all nations; and then the end will come" (Matthew 24:14). His expectation of the soon-return of the Lord Jesus Christ prompted the question: what can I do to contribute? A vision was born out of Matt. 24:14—a vision to mobilize the church in India, and particularly the historic churches of which his father was one of the first bishops, a vision to implement a seven-step plan to reach every lost and last of the unreached nations or people groups of India. Viji is the regional coordinator of Partners International for South Asia. They have adopted this project and are calling it "Vision India."

A second example from a different region of the world is the case of Dr. Hyung-Ja Lee, President of the Torch Center in Korea. When approached about hosting the GCOWE '95 conference in Seoul, she responded favorably and became a great supporter not only of the event itself but of the vision coming out of the event.

I will never forget the day my wife Doris and I walked into her office just prior to GCOWE '95. We came to thank her for the incredible amount of time, effort, funds, and the readjusting of the entire layout of parts of the center to accommodate an office for GCOWE, for both the Korean preparation staff and the AD2000 international staff for about a year. Why did she do this? We asked her. Her quiet answer came, spoken spontaneously with strong conviction, "To hasten the Lord's return, and I believe this will help."

A third example from another region of the world, and a different context, occurred recently as a small group met to discuss relationships in light of much transition in the years ahead from WEF, the Lausanne Committee, and the AD2000 & Beyond Movement. As the group reflected from the Scriptures about the future, Hilde Fjeldstad, rector of the Lutheran Bible Seminary in Norway and executive committee member for the Lausanne Committee for some ten years, shared her thoughts introduced by the words, "I believe this relates a lot to things we are working on." She then quoted from a Norwegian hymn the words of Russian composer Lvov and prayed, "Lord help us remember that you are coming back soon...reconciliation is needed...leadership is needed...gather the harvest."

God-Given Vision is Exploding

If a vision for God's purposes is a thermometer of spiritual vitality, as suggested by the following verses in Scripture, this is a most encouraging trend. In Proverbs 29:18 (KJV) we read, "Where there is no vision, the people perish." When Samuel was just a boy at the end of the era of the judges in Israel, when everybody was doing what was right in their own eyes, Scripture reports: "In those days the word of the Lord was rare; there were not many visions" (I Samuel 3:1b).

All kind of vision based on the Word of God is proliferating. These are visions of many types; by Christians from within a country, in local settings, by region, by city, by neighborhood, by people group, by denomination, by Christian organization.

For example, the Friends Missionary Prayer Band in India has developed "Hindi Heartland Penetration Strategies" to mobilize 1000 new missionaries to research and to evangelize 300 unreached people groups within the next few years.

India Reach is a mission to reap a spiritual harvest in India. Their mission is to reach 500 million people with the Gospel of Jesus Christ by the year 2000 by generating direct mail responses from media, and to organize personal visitors to the individuals who respond, within six weeks of their response. They are believing God for over 85 million decisions for Christ by the year 2000. A key component is the development of partnerships mutually relating and working together with different churches, ministries, and Christian organizations that have a common mission to reach India with the gospel message. Steering committees for follow-up are being chaired by different denominational and Christian organization leaders in twelve major cities.

The Evangelical Church of India has a denominational plan to establish 1000 local churches by then. With almost 900 churches already, they expect to reach their goal in 1998—two years ahead of schedule.

The examples go on and on. In fact, at the time of GCOWE '95, Indian church historian S. D. Ponraj prepared a book on the specific plans by recognized Christian ministries in India with a target date of the year 2000. They numbered 150. Now he reports these have grown to 200, representing hundreds of thousands of workers and hundreds of thousands of churches. Not only are there individual visions and plans, but they are increasingly networked into joint strategies.

Indigenous Networked Strategies are Increasing

Increasingly indigenous ministries are working together. To reach the region of North India, key Christian leaders, lay people, medical doctors, engineers, and scientists representing many different organizations and churches have come together as the North India Harvest Network to reach North India. They use a catchy phrase "PLUG, PREM, and be NICE" in which the acronym PREM summarizes these various methods and means "love" in the Hindi language.

*PLUG answers the question, "Who are we reaching in church planting?"*When we talk of saturation church planting, most of us have a single approach in mind. It is usually a geographical approach or a city strategy or a people group strategy. Actually none of these strategies is all inclusive. They are overlapping and complementary. PLUG indicates the targets they are trying to reach: every PEOPLE in every

LANGUAGE in every URBAN center in every GEOGRAPHIC division (district, block, and PIN code). Much like a net, each target group serves as a thread woven from a different direction to ensure that every fish (person) is caught (comes to Christ) regardless of the language they speak, the cultural grouping they are a part of, the city in which they reside, or the geographical district where they are found. Different people and organizations in and outside of India are invited to adopt one or more of these groups with the view of reaching every people group in every language in every city and every district.

How do we reach them? Through PREM and NICE. There are numerous ways we can reach people. At least four are essential.

(1) **Prayer** is the key and the center of the strategy, and the only way the task can be done. Anybody trying to do evangelism without undergirding their efforts with believing, importunate prayer, even with the clear mandate of the Great Commission, is attempting the fruitless.

(2) **Research** into the harvest field helps us to identify the unfinished task. It also helps us to know where the harvest force is. Our prayers and our efforts need to be informed if prayer is to be effective. In the past Christians ignored research. We can do that no longer.

(3) **Mobilization** is necessary. The harvest force needs to be mobilized. The harvest is truly plenteous and the laborers are few. We need to pray and mobilize believers everywhere.

(4) **Equipping** is a must. The harvest force needs to be equipped to meet the challenge. Massive training should be done to empower them.

Both PLUG and PREM have coordinators with a committee that seeks to implement strategic input.

NICE refers to how to go about the task: by **networking** (something of special importance in pioneering situations), by taking **initiative** when nothing is happening or a gap is realized, by being a **catalyst** (an agent that provokes or speeds significant change or action) and by **encouraging** all the existing ministries and initiatives from within and without that advance the cause of Jesus Christ in the area.

Indigenous Christian Leadership is Emerging throughout the Two-Thirds World

In his farewell speech as the Dean of the School of World Missions at Fuller, Paul Pearson spoke on trends in mission today. He had pointed out decades ago the emergence of Two-Thirds World missions as the great new fact of our age. In his later remarks he noted the emergence of Christian leadership from the Two-Thirds World as a key factor in our time.

Just yesterday the Moody Radio station was announcing an inter-view with Dr. David Kim, Pastor of the Alleluia Church in Korea, on the subject of Christian leadership. David Kim is the Consultation Director for the Consultation for Presidents and Academic Deans to be held as one of the nine parallel consultations at GCOWE '97 in South Africa. David is currently teaching an intensive course on Christian leadership at Trinity International University in nearby Deerfield, Illinois.

For years David has been a student of leadership. He has studied the lives of 150 secular leaders seeking an answer to the question, "What made them successful?" He has also studied biblical leaders and church leaders and has been a student of the emerging leadership of the Korean church. He relates that the first three characteristics of a successful leader are: (1) a clear vision, (2) a detailed plan, and (3) action following the plan, based on the vision. This is precisely what can be observed among leaders of indigenous ministries worldwide today.

The Internationalization of Sponsorship of Indigenous Ministries

Korea moved out of the category of debtor nations a year ago. A year later, funds have been authorized by the government to be sent out of the country for legitimate purposes, including support of Chris-tian ministries. Strategies for reaching unreached peoples and advanc-ing the cause of Christ in the world include not only the sending of missionaries from Korea but the financial support of indigenous min-istries worldwide.

In a session on evaluation of Joshua Project 2000 by Christian church and mission leaders in Singapore working in small groups, what became clear was the readiness of the Singapore church not only to send missionaries but to partner with indigenous ministries as well.

The 6,000-plus Chinese churches in the Diaspora are becoming a factor increasingly in the support of indigenous ministries around the world.

We are living in a day in which, although the Christian wealth continues to reside mainly in the West and particularly in the U. S., increasingly other parts of the world are eager to be partnering with indigenous ministries.

Support of Indigenous Ministries Has Become Conventional Rather Than Radical

It normally takes a generation to institutionalize and move from radical to conventional. Forty years ago supporting national efforts was radical. Today it is conventional. As we meet at this consultation, we are experiencing the institutionalization of a good idea. There are more than 100 organizations committed to a primary mission of supporting indigenous ministries—some forty of them at this consultation.

I am happy to note that some of the pioneers are being honored now, receiving honor where honor is due. I believe this also honors the Lord. The pioneers faced tremendous opposition to establish the ministerial legitimacy of the empowerment of national ministries.

At the same time, as we look back to the exchange between the Lord and his followers, it strikes me that his way appears continuously to be the radical way. Does that call us to some kinds of abandonment, as we think of the conventionality of what this approach to ministry has become?

The passage used earlier from Luke also calls us to consider another trend that may not be comforting.

Transactional Approach Rather Than Transformational

As support of indigenous ministries has been conducted, increasingly the tendency is more to a transactional rather than a transformational approach to working out the partnership relationship. We talk of industry standards. We put a strong emphasis on accountability, policies, and procedures. These are undoubtedly necessary. Yet with greater emphasis, they tend toward a transactional approach for partnership (trading this for that) rather than a transformational approach.

Rather than moving toward more control, is there not a call to fewer controls? Is that not what indigenous ministries are calling for? Is that not what donors are calling for? Is that not what the advance of technology is moving toward—from the boat to the plane, to phone, to fax, to E-mail, to the Web? Communication is becoming increasingly and directly interactive between donor and indigenous ministry, with fewer agencies in between.

The transformational approach would be to bring to bear the full impact of God's breakthrough and the spiritual vitalization of a people in one culture to another culture. In my view, one of the greatest hopes for the church in the West is transformation through exposure to what the Spirit of God is doing in the non-Western world.

As we reflect upon the provocative nature and kingdom value of servanthood and radical Christianity that excited our Lord in Luke 22, here is another trend worthy of our consideration.

**Emphasis on the Rational Rather Than the Relational Nature
of Support for Indigenous Ministries**

We can do this the way the "world" does it. However, the Lord has
shown us that the way forward is on the basis of fellowship and trust.
The key biblical word is "koinonia," translated in Philippians 1 as
partnership, normally referring to the precious fellowship we share
because we are one in Christ.

This attitude then leads us to the radical step of seeking to be
servants rather than merely partners—serving those at the table, rather
than sitting with them. In Luke 22:24–30 (for whatever reason) their
attitude was that of the world, where competition and authority are
important to success. In the kingdom of God, greatness is measured by
how many you serve, not how many serve you. Jesus is the model for
our ministry, and He was a servant.

If relationship is so important then it leads to the constant need for
reconciliation and the spiritual intermingling that accompanies it.

Conclusion

The words of a Norwegian hymn sum up the heart cry of so many
of our indigenous ministry partners: "Rise up, O church of God. He is
now calling, the night is over, the day is shining bright. Freedom He
brought you, He who soon is coming. Be glad you church of God,
rejoice in your calling. Gather the flock…Great is the harvest…Great is
the need for workers…soon He will be calling. The Bridegroom is
coming. Then He will bring you home."

The Lord assured them that the greatest glory was yet to come
(Luke 22:29–30). How do we move into that, beyond the transient glory
of this world? May this volume add great fabric and spirit to help
answer this question.

CHAPTER 3

The Kingdom Forcefully Advances
What the Future Holds for the Indigenous Movement

William Taylor

Earlier this year when I was in Singapore, I asked my taxi driver how things were going in Singapore. I like talking to taxi drivers because they have a real perspective on reality. This elderly Chinese man said, "I have no eye to look-see, but I think Red China is going to take Hong Kong, and then they are going to take Taiwan. And then Malaysia is going to take Singapore. I have no eye to look-see, but I think." It was a rather disturbing prophecy.

As we think about the future of our movement, that's how I feel. I have no eye to look-see, but I think. And we must think globally, with a wide-angle lens, and we must try to see our Lord's perspective on the future of missions.

There is a pregnant passage that comes out of our Lord's dialog in Matthew 11. Jesus said in verse 12, "From the days of John the Baptist until now, the kingdom of heaven has been forcefully advancing, and forceful men lay hold of it." This pregnant little phrase has some decided ambiguities in it which I will mine for all they are worth. What was Jesus saying? He rooted it in time, from the days of John the Baptist until now. John...Jesus ...Messiah. The kingdom of heaven. The invisible invasion from on high has been forcefully advancing through the teachings of John...through the prophetic denunciations of John...through the teachings and the miracles and the prophetic denunciations of our Lord Himself. There was a forceful advance and I think it refers to physical force as well as spiritual force.

As we think of the global scenario today, we are privileged to live in a day of forceful advance of the kingdom of heaven. The last 30 to 35 years are a stunning account. I live in Austin, Texas, and our three children have gone to the University of Texas. I love that university atmosphere because if the Christian faith does not work on that campus, it won't work anywhere. In a recent open-air meeting, one of the accusations was that Christianity is a Western religion. In reply, the

Inter-Varsity evangelist on campus for that week gave an astounding documentation on the status of the Church of Jesus Christ in Africa, Asia, and Latin America. And God has allowed you and me to live at this time of history.

There are more believers today in Asia than there are in all of the Western nations of Europe, North America, Australia, and New Zealand. The majority of that number are in China. But we also know that the enemy is alive and well and operating in all kinds of false teachings. So the kingdom of heaven is advancing forcefully. And you and I are part of it.

But it's the second phrase that's the tough one—where the ambiguity lies. "Forceful men lay hold of it." This has two sides to it. Number one, some translations say, "The kingdom of heaven suffers violence and the violent ones conquer it." The New American Standard Bible reads, "The kingdom suffers violence, and violent men take it by force." But the Moffett New Testament says, "They are pressing into the realm of heaven." These eager souls are storming in. This gives a different perspective. The RSV says, "The kingdom of heaven has suffered violence and men of violence take it by force." The Living Bible says, "The ardent multitudes have been crowding towards the kingdom of heaven."

Do you see the ambiguity? It is one of two, or both, and I think it's both. I think Jesus has given us a decided ambiguity that as the advance of the kingdom of heaven is experienced, two things happen. The bold ones say, "I want to be a part of it." They are the forceful men and women who say, "I want to be a part of this bold, forceful advance of the kingdom of heaven." The other side is that as the kingdom advances forcefully, the violent ones will oppose it violently. And we have many illustrations of the violence against the gospel in Asia, Africa, and Latin America. This is a century of unprecedented persecution of Christians. The stories of violence are many and ugly.

We who live in the West seem to think that the kingdom of heaven cannot advance unless we have peace and prosperity…and connections. But what Scripture tells us, and what history teaches us, is that those are not the conditions for the advance.

As I observe the world scene, I see significant changes taking place.

Changes That Affect Our Ministries

1. The first is the three major political economic blocks that are emerging on the scene—the Pacific Rim, North America (particularly after NAFTA), and greater Europe. This brings the whole concept of

the borderless world—the borderless economy—and the massive transactions of financial resources every day through electronic switches. When we think of those wealthy or economic blocks, we wonder where the rest of the world is. Where does Latin America fit? Where is Africa? Where are the less-advantaged, or less-developed, nations of Asia? Are they simply cheap labor? It is ironic that it is in these areas where the kingdom of heaven seems to be advancing the strongest. It is as if God repeatedly turns the tables on us.

2. Next, look at the rogue nations, the rebel nations, the hard-to-control ones such as Iraq, Iran, and Afghanistan. Religious and political fundamentalisms fuse those together. At the root is not just Islamic fundamentalism; it's an ethnicity that drives it. What would happen if a rogue nation like Iran sealed a deal for six nuclear weapons from one of the former Central Asia republics? Or worse yet, a splinter faction of the Palestinian movement got a nuclear warhead!

3. Another component in the world global scene is neotribalism, which has a vicious and violent span. Look at the former Yugoslavia, now in seven pieces. Or the battles in Sri Lanka and many countries of Africa, to say nothing about Rwanda, Burundi, and Zaire.

4. Then changing the scenario—the fourth component in the global scene is the radical information revolution. An October 1996 issue of *US News & World Report* featured the release of a book called *24 Hours in Cyberspace.* This fascinating article is provocative and very disturbing. "Cyberspace—a world in which communities are no longer limited to physical location. That is now the real world. The marketplace…the battleground…the house of prayer…and the secret retreat." The religious illustration accompanying the article was a picture of two Buddhist monks worshiping before Lord Buddha, and then tapping into the computer as they spread their message to evangelize the masses. What bothers me is why did *US News & World Report* use the Buddhists as the example? Why not somebody representing the Christian faith?

How does the radical information revolution affect us? Well, it is no longer a matter of smuggling Bibles—it's CDs containing all the translations and commentaries in whatever language one wants. This is with the assumption, of course, that the people to whom we smuggle the CDs have a CD-ROM and the technology. But that will come and with it, new vocabulary… new technology…new categories.

5. Then there is the spread of modernity and secularization—a close cousin to modernity—the post-modern world view. It does not surprise me to see this philosophy in Europe or North America. But what is striking is to see how this idea is spreading throughout Latin

America, the continent with which I am most familiar. Yet with the fall of the Marxist European and the Russian system in Latin America, the dominant political commitment of university students in Latin America is that there is nothing worth living for or dying for. There is a malaise of pessimism on the campuses, and that pessimism is part of a philosophical movement. I am convinced that it is rippling all through the Pacific Rim.

We who have been cross-cultural missionaries unwittingly have brought in our perspectives on modernity and technology. For example, if we are in a nation with scarce resources in medicine, and our daughter gets seriously ill, our instinctive first question is, "How far away is the doctor?" And then when we get the doctor and the medicine, we ask God to guide the doctor and bless the medicine. Whereas our colleague who loves God equally would say, "Why not first start with God and ask Him to heal?" We have unwittingly slipped in a world view that is not necessarily biblical.

6. Another powerful force emerging is the militant world religions and Western spiritualities. The New Age is a marvelous melange of East and West. One can be material and spiritual at the same time. We see not only the missionary vision of Islam, but Hinduism and Buddhism also.

7. Then there is the globalization of the Church of Jesus Christ. The Holy Spirit is the traveling member of the Trinity and He is doing a lot of work where people are responding, but it is an uneven growth. Some parts of Indonesia are much more open to the gospel; other parts are very closed. The same is true with the Philippines, India, Africa, and Latin America. People think that the whole continent of Latin America is turning to Jesus Christ in its evangelical variety. That is not the case. In Uruguay the predominant statement is agnosticism or atheism, thanks to the European immigrants. But praise God, the Holy Spirit has not abandoned us wherever we are.

8. Something else on the rise is the globalized international church with a global vision. There is a new equation of giftings, of human and material resources. A North/South/East/West learning school. New international leadership and leadership styles. My boss is Jun Vencer, a Filipino lawyer/management expert/Christian Missionary Alliance pastor. One of the great challenges in our small leadership team is understanding each other because we come from different nationalities. How does Jun make decisions? How does he analyze? This has been a tremendous growth curve for all of us, and for Jun in trying to understand us. I am this peculiar hybrid of a missionary kid from Latin

America who spent 30 years in Latin America, and I live in my passport country—the United States. What does it mean to work under someone who is not from my culture? That is one of the global scenario components.

9. Then there is the paradox of weakness and strength of the Western and non-Western church. Unfortunately we have pitted the church in North America, for example, against the church in Latin America or Africa or Asia. As if it is all evil or all management by objectives in North America, and the Holy Spirit really sort of checked out. Whereas in these other continents, God is really alive. This is a dangerous oversimplification.

As I travel across the United States, God has shown me a lot of churches with a powerful commitment to the leading of the Holy Spirit. They are doing something right because people are coming to faith in Jesus Christ and are being equipped. In no country is the church all glowing and marvelous. And in no country is it all negative. We have to realize this as we think globally.

10. And the last item I'll mention on the changing global scene is the organized, as well as spontaneous, persecution of the Church. The World Evangelical Fellowship calls an annual world day of prayer for the persecuted Church. The response is astonishing. In Bulgaria more than a thousand churches were praying for the persecuted Christians in Bulgaria. In scores of countries around the world there is a sense that we must intercede for our brothers and sisters.

There is the rise of the martyrs. I cannot fully understand that incredible passage in Revelation 6:9–11 where John peers under the altar and sees the souls of those who had given their blood on account of the Word and their testimony. John saw them. They cry out with a loud voice and say, "Holy despot, sovereign Lord. How long until you avenge our blood?" There are two responses. First, they are all given white robes. Big deal. Here is a new change of clothing for you. But in the context of the book of Revelation we see what that robe represents. It is a beautiful gift. It's not that they are just lining up for some massive martyrs' choir. Then, secondly, they are told to wait because the number is not complete.

Someone has said that there are more martyrs this century for the cause of Christ than in all the previous centuries combined—somewhere around 119 million martyrs just in this century. Well, how big is that little cavity under the altar? Are they expanding the room for more martyrs?

Heart Talk to the Indigenous Movement

There is a great saying in Spanish, "speak with my heart in my hand." I would like to do this now. I have an overwhelming sense that the sovereign God wants to pour out His blessing on you, and on our movement...because we are a movement for the future. God wants to pour out His blessing, but are we ready to receive? I have four concerns about this. The first two would be on the more negative side—the second two more positive.

Beware of Looking at the World through a Straw

What does it mean to look at the world through a straw? This is a reductionism. It's "us versus them." "I'm a little guy but I am a humble little guy, and all those are big guys." Or we have national ministries and not any other kind of ministries. That can be a "straw." Or colonial versus native missionaries—that's another "straw." Or our church only accepts people who come out of our church and are approved and equipped here; we do not take anybody who is a graduate of a seminary. More straws. Or we are 10/40 window people. Or West versus non-West. Straws.

We have to put on glasses that will give us a better perspective. So beware of straws. Beware of reductionisms that we tend to create for self-affirmation. If I can reduce the world to what I see in a straw, then that is the only world that exists for me, but it is a dangerous perspective.

Ethics and Accountability

All of us know there are fraudulent schemers in our movement. A friend of mine some years ago said, "Bill, Haiti is a huge sinkhole of American money." Ebenezer Sunderaj, one of my colleagues, head of the India Missions Association, has been a good resource for me because periodically, due to my relationship with WEF and the Missions Commission, either churches or some person will call and say, "What do you know about such-and-such a ministry in India?" I say, "Well, let me ask Ebenezer." He has given me good counsel. And maybe he says, "Oh, that brother is quite well known, but not for the good things." Hong Kong is another great sinkhole. Russia is a marvelous one now. And starving children anywhere. These may all be worthy causes, but when they are used by the scam artists, those of us who are in this long term and for good, get stung also.

Another observation is that we have to be careful how we work the motivations of our donor base. Do we use guilt? Pictures of starving kids shown in the context of very wealthy churches will generate money, but it may be guilt money.

In our advertising, are we sensationalizing our stories in our desire to get across our message? The pictures we show of our ministry. Is that one church of 5,000 where I once spoke part of our ministry? The people back in the donor base say, "My goodness! Look at how God is blessing Brother or Sister so-and-so. They have 5,000 just in one church." So we misrepresent reality, and we exaggerate our impact.

In writing proposals, foundations want to know, "What are your outcomes? As a result of this grant of $300 or $300,000, what will be your global outputs?" They want us to quantify. So in our desire to get that grant, do we create mythical, quantifiable outcomes that do not happen?

Now another observation in a different direction is that people in the Western or North American churches want to get more impact for their dollar. So in some cases we may "rent" a national because it is cheaper. We say for the cost of one North American missionary, we can get 100 native missionaries, or national workers. In our movement we can feed this because we can give them a cost analysis. This is neocolonialism—a phony evangelical imperialism. And again, it creates a false dichotomy.

Yet another observation—what do we say about each other confidentially? Or let's put the shoe on Bill Taylor. I work with World Evangelical Fellowship. What do I say about AD 2000 and Beyond? Or what do I say about the Lausanne Movement? We need to come up with a covenant that will curb our tongues.

A final matter under this problematic ethics subhead comes when we portray the West as the sole source of money. In Brazil some years ago I was on a quasi-board of a ministry that raises money for homeless children in Brazil. The missions pastor of a megachurch in the United States and I were meeting with some Brazilians who were on the Brazilian board of this ministry that was struggling to raise about $75,000 from the USA. We went to a reception in a Brazilian apartment that turned out to be two entire floors of that complex. The owner was a prominent professional in that city. Another guest was a prominent national banker who was worth, I was told, $150 million. Another guest was a high industrialist. And they were talking about how they could raise $75,000 in North America. They asked my opinion. All of a sudden I realized that they did not really want to hear my opinion because my opinion was that they could raise $500,000 right there in that room. I was overwhelmed. I have not been around that much wealth in the USA.

When I go to Korea I see the mega-edifice complex of some churches, unlike any I have seen this side of Korea. We need to remember that there is money in places besides the West.

Discovering a Sense of the Body of Christ

We need each other! Maybe I run a little "mom and pop" operation. Maybe it's "me, myself, and I." Or maybe our church has an international division. It may have a separate incorporation, or it may be part of the missionary budget and called something else. Then we have some creative, restless boomers who are entrepreneurs and who have a different idea how to do things. Whatever it is, we need each other. And that means we need to listen to each other.

As we listen to and learn from each other, we can then determine what not to do. Pumping money into a national ministry can sometimes be the greatest curse for that ministry. I read of a small denomination in the former Soviet Republics that received a grant for $1.5 million. That was the worst thing that could have happened to them. We need to discover the Body of Christ to see the role that West and non-West, North and South—all the players—have.

Concrete Steps in the Right Direction

First is that we would commit to verbally and tangibly affirm each other. Another, that we will not slice up the same donor by making our ministry appear more significant than someone else.

Second, we need to develop some kind of shared values and standards. I don't want to say "industry standards" because as Luis Bush said, we must be careful about *transactional* things versus *transformational* things. Perhaps we can run our publicity ideas—our pictures, our advertising—by another colleague in our movement. "What do you think of this picture or this idea?"

Third, we men and women need to have a significant accountability relationship with somebody. And building on the accountability idea, we need to make sure that the ministries we support have a field-based accountability.

On July 5, 1994 in Singapore, our WEF staff signed an agreement committing ourselves to seven things—personal purity, the spiritual disciplines, to family, to the local church, to financial integrity, not to criticize others in the Body, and to honest communication.

We return now to the ultimate of ultimates and realize that the most important thing for the church is not evangelism. The ultimate goal for us in our movement is not reaching the unreached. The ultimate goal is worship. When this age is over and the countless millions of the redeemed fall on their faces before the throne of God, missions will be no more. But worship abides forever. In missions we simply aim to bring the nations into white-hot enjoyment of God's glory.

May the peoples praise you, O God; may all the peoples praise you. May the nations be glad and sing for joy (Psalm 67:3–4a).

CHAPTER 4

Incarnational Presence
Dependency and Interdependency in Overseas Partnerships

David Howard

My wife and I went back to Colombia in December 1995. The association that started in 1945 was celebrating its fiftieth anniversary. They invited many of us who had served there to come back to celebrate with them. In 1958, there were only twelve organized churches and maybe twenty-five congregations in that association. There are now 500 churches. They were forced into independence back in the '50s. They had to take over and do it themselves, and they have done it beautifully. Not one missionary was involved in planning or directing the anniversary celebration. They asked me to speak every night and I was glad to do that. But the point is, they ran the show. This turns our thoughts to our topic—*dependency and interdependency in overseas partnerships.*

First, I want to express my deep appreciation to the leaders and founders of the movement of partnering with nationals. At times, I confess I have had vacillations in my own feelings about how such a movement should go in terms of helping and supporting national workers in other parts of the world. I come from a mission not involved primarily in supporting national pastors and other workers. However, we have many non-Westerners in our mission. We have a number of Latins who are missionaries of the Latin America Mission. Our mission was one of the first to do that kind of thing back when Dr. Kenneth Strachen was general director years ago.

The two words—*dependency* and *interdependency*—will be keys to our understanding. But first, a few words about terminology. I appreciated Luis Bush giving us that long list of possible definitions for the word *indigenous*. Certain words have also been frequently used in the mission context here that I consider not helpful. However, I cannot find better words myself, so I cannot offer suggestions. For example, the words *nationals* or *native missionaries*. I am a native missionary, because I am a native of North America and I went as a missionary to Latin

America. That makes me a native missionary: native from my country. Or I am a national missionary. I am a national of this country—I went to another country in cross-cultural missions. So that terminology—though I know what we mean by it—is not fully descriptive.

Then look at the term *colonial missionaries*. That pejorative term has weighted implications, and nearly always creates negative implications. It is not a helpful term because it puts me, and others, into a negative position—a colonial missionary.

Another phrase sometimes used is the term *authentic missionary*. This always refers to those who are the so-called indigenous or national missionaries in other countries. They are the *authentic* ones. I have never heard Western missionaries called *unauthentic*, but the implication is clearly there. If certain missionaries from one part of the world are *authentic*, then those who come from another part of the world must be *unauthentic*. I clearly resent that. I have spent my entire life in missionary work, and the idea that I am unauthentic offends me. It is not constructive to think in those terms.

I have been involved in the sending aspect nearly all my life. First, I went as a foreign missionary to Latin America for fifteen years. Inter-Varsity then asked me to return to the States as Missions Director and to head the Urbana conventions. Thus for ten years of my life, I was involved in recruiting others to send them as missionaries. That is what Urbana and the missions thrust of Inter-Varsity is all about. Then I was invited into the World Evangelical Fellowship, which specializes in cooperative work all over the world with national churches and evangelical alliances. So I have been involved from that angle. Now I am back with the Latin America Mission, where again I am involved in sending. My entire life has been spent in this type of ministry.

I want to start with a *biblical basis*, then give some *historical background*, and finally talk about the *present situation*, as I see it, of dependency and interdependency.

Biblical Basis

It is not my intention nor my assignment today to give an exegetical study of New Testament passages. However, I think it would be proper to refer to a few well known passages.

I Corinthians 12 is the primary passage about interdependency within the Body of Christ.

> Now the body is not made up of one part but of many. If the
> foot should say, "Because I am not a hand, I do not belong

to the body," it would not for that reason cease to be a part of the body. And if the ear should say, "Because I am not an eye, I do not belong to the body," it would not for that reason cease to be part of the body. If the whole body were an eye, where would the sense of hearing be? If the whole body were an ear, where would the sense of smell be? But in fact God has arranged the parts of the body, every one of them, just as He wanted them to be. If they were all one part, where would the body be? As it is, there are many parts, but one body. The eye cannot say to the hand, "I don't need you!" And the head cannot say to the feet, "I don't need you." On the contrary, those parts of the body that seem to be weaker are indispensable, and the parts that we think are less honorable we treat with special honor (I Corinthians 12:14–23a).

This is the most significant passage in the New Testament about our interdependency. It is impossible for us to say, "I do not need you." An eye cannot hear. An ear cannot see. If the ear is going to see, it needs the help of the eye. If the eye is going to hear, it needs the help of the ear. Interdependency within the Body of Christ is absolutely foundational to our work.

One other passage is Galatians 6 where, by the way, the King James version is not very helpful. Two verses seem contradictory in the King James translation. Galatians 6:2 says: *Carry each other's burdens, and in this way you will fulfill the law of Christ.* In verse 5, the KJV says: *Every man should carry his own burden.* The problem arises because of improper translation. The two words used for *burden*, in verse 2 and in verse 5, are not the same words in Greek. In verse 2 the Greek word is *ta baray,* which means "a weight or heaviness or something grievous to be born." We should carry that with the other person.

K. P. Yohannan gives a marvelous testimony of the heaviness of the burden, of carrying the work in so many places—the persecutions—the dangers—all that goes into carrying the burden of world evangelization. We have to carry this together. No one person can carry it alone.

Then Galatians 6:5 says: *Each one should carry his own load.* The NIV does not use the same word, rightly so, because the Greek word there is *to phortion,* which means "a burden of imposed precepts or responsibilities." Each should carry his or her own responsibility. There are matters we must care for ourselves and not cast on someone else. One of those responsibilities is world evangelization. I can help the other person carry it, but I also have to carry my part. So each must carry his or her own burden.

Historical Background of Missions

I find it helpful in our context to classify modern mission history in three eras: *dependence, independence,* and *interdependence.*

Era of Dependence. I arbitrarily date that from 1793 to 1945 and I will explain why. Seventeen ninety-three (1793) was the year William Carey arrived in India. Most mission historians date the modern movement from that point. Throughout that era there was the dependence of the national church on those who had brought the gospel to them in the first place. That dependence was inevitable.

It was indispensable that those who had the gospel take it to those who did not have it. Those who were getting it for the first time obviously were dependent on those who brought it to them, just as children are dependent on their parents. There was no way out of that. But it lasted far too long, until 1945 (the end of World War II) when we moved into an entirely new era—politically, economically, sociologically, and in missions as well. The world was changed forever after World War II.

Era of Independence. The dates I assign here are 1945 to 1974. This was the era when the great colonial empires were collapsing all over the world. The British Empire collapsed. The Italian Empire had already collapsed. The French and Portuguese Empires were collapsing. Of course we have to say in parenthesis that another great empire was growing—the Soviet Empire. They never wanted to call themselves an empire, but they were as imperialistic as anyone had ever been. That empire was growing while the other empires were collapsing. New nations were rising in Africa and elsewhere. Along with that, there was the independence movement of the national churches. They were also rising and saying, "It is time for us to be handling things ourselves." The "missionary go home" idea came along in that period. "Get out! Leave us to ourselves!"

Then came the call by the World Council in the early '70s: "Let's call a *moratorium.* Do not send missionaries for a while. Let them take over by themselves." There was some justification for that movement, because the dependency had lasted far too long. It was right that the independence attitude should come, and fortunately, it did.

Era of Interdependence. This era dates from 1974 to the present. Why 1974? That was the date of the first Lausanne Congress. I pay tribute to those who organized that congress and what came out of it. I think the Lausanne Covenant is one of the few statements that has really made an impact.

At Lausanne, Donald McGavran and Ralph Winter shocked the world of missions. Prior to Lausanne, most mission leaders were thinking that we were very close to finishing the job of world evangelization. Geographically, the gospel had advanced to practically every corner of the earth. Those pockets of closed countries where the church did not exist yet were few in terms of the overall geography of the world.

Donald McGavran and Ralph Winter said, "True, the gospel has gone geographically to most places, but what about the people groups? We have been thinking geographically too long. The gospel has gone here, here, here, but what about all those people groups?" They came up with the figure (rightly or wrongly) of 2.7 billion unreached peoples, which was the figure quoted extensively afterwards. Subsequently there have been studies and statistics to try to figure out who really is unreached and how to define unreached peoples. The point is, they alerted the world of missions to the fact that the job still had a long way to go before we could say that world evangelization is coming to its completion.

So what does this mean? This means that the job is far too big for any one group, church, organization, or country to do alone. There must be *interdependence* in the Body of Christ to reach those as yet unreached.

The Present Situation

I will share personal experience here to illustrate how I see the situation. In 1937 the Latin America Mission opened a ministry in Northern Colombia and began planting churches. In 1945, these churches organized their own national church association, which basically was like a denomination for Colombia. However, the Mission was still very much involved with them.

When I got there in 1958, I discovered there was a ten-year plan in effect. The ten-year plan stated that every year, the Mission subsidy to those churches should be cut 10 percent. At the end of ten years, the churches would be totally independent financially. They were about five or six years along in this plan when I arrived. I was asked to be the field director, which meant that I had to have the oversight of everything that we as a Mission were doing in that region. It was not long before the church leaders came to me and said, "This ten-year plan...you know, it is not really going to work. By the time this plan has phased itself out, there is no way we are going to be able to handle things ourselves. Why don't we rethink this? Give it another ten years. Okay?"

I was influenced then by the writings of Donald McGavran's early book, *Bridges of God*. It had a tremendous impact on my life in thinking through some of these things. If we revised the ten-year plan and started over, we would never reach the proper kind of independence followed by interdependence. What they needed was independence. So we stood our ground. The churches were not very happy with that, but it worked.

When my wife and I returned for the fiftieth anniversary celebration, it was thrilling to see what God had done. They were effusive in expressing appreciation to the missionaries. This is a new generation. The older generation was often resentful about missionaries who had controlled things. However, the new generation has come along and said, "We are your great-grandchildren. Thank you for coming. Thank you for making it possible for us to do what we are doing today." I am so glad that we did not give in to their request to revise the ten-year plan and keep helping them out. They have done far better on their own.

This affected local churches also. In 1958 one of my first tasks was turning over to the national church the properties that legally belonged to the Latin America Mission. The Mission had bought these properties, built churches, and held many of their legal deeds. We decided it was the proper time to put them into the hands of the churches.

I remember one church built by missionaries with money they had received. There was only a handful of people in the church. In Spanish we say *cuatro gatos*—"four cats" basically formed the congregation. The time had come to tell them, "This is your church. You take the deed and the property and all responsibilities with it."

They said, "Thank you. That is great. Will you please continue to pay the taxes and the maintenance?"

We replied, "Absolutely not! If the church is yours, it is yours, and we will not pay for that."

Some of them were incensed. "You mean you are not going to pay the taxes anymore?"

"No!"

There were struggles in those days, but it was part of the independence movement, so that later we could become interdependent.

In almost every church where a missionary was attending, the missionary served as the treasurer, handling the funds. I thought,

"Wait a minute, what is wrong here? Can't these churches have their own treasurers? Do missionaries have to handle the funds?" One day a pastor came to me and complained that he had not been paid yet. That was none of my business. I had nothing to do with his salary. His church was independent. So I said, "Why haven't you been paid?" He replied, "The señorita did not pay me." The señorita happened to be my secretary, a missionary. In his mind, the medium was the message and the message was, "The Mission is paying me." Thus he complained to me that he had not been paid yet. We had nothing to do with his salary except that one of our missionaries happened to be handling that local church's funds, and there were not enough to pay him yet. I thought, "Wow! This is bad news."

So I sent out an order to all of our missionaries saying, "No more missionaries as treasurers after six months. You can train a Colombian for six months and then turn it over."

Fortunately, they all did. Not long afterwards one church began to lose some funds. They found out that the treasurer was misusing funds. They replaced him and it was not long before the new person was doing the same thing. They named a third, and he did the same thing. Finally, they came to me in desperation and said, "You have to give us a missionary. We are losing money."

I asked, "Why are you are losing money?"

"Well, the treasurers got away with it."

I replied, "That is not my problem. That is *your* problem. You have to learn how to handle your own money. We are not going to do that for you." They were upset that we would not give them a missionary to handle their funds.

Today that church is a booming church with no missionary support at all. The independence had to come so that we can now have interdependence.

By contrast, when I first arrived in Colombia, we discovered that a most amazing grass roots people movement was taking place out in the backwoods. This was while the persecution was still very rampant in Colombia. That persecution period, known as *La Violencia*—the violence—lasted for some fifteen years in Colombia. Vicious, violent persecution arose against evangelical Protestants—pastors imprisoned, churches burned, schools closed, children of evangelicals beaten up on the street, people killed. There may have been more than 120 martyrs in Colombia during those days, but we can statistically prove at least 120 who died for their faith.

Suddenly a spontaneous combustion people movement was taking place out in the jungle areas. I went into that area to find out what
was happening. We, as a Mission, had nothing to do with starting it. It
was ignited by a spark of the Holy Spirit. These people were witnessing
to everybody. God laid His hand on one man in particular, Victor
Landero. Victor led his whole family to the Lord—nine brothers and
sisters, father and mother. He planted a church that grew so well that
he moved off to another area, bought a plot of land, and started a
second church.

The first time I went to his village, ninety-four people were living
there—ninety-two of them now Christians. He was working on the
other two. Victor had no relationship to the Mission except to ask us,
"Can you come and help us understand the Bible?" These people were
largely illiterate. Victor Landero himself had never been to first grade,
much less Bible school or seminary. He did know how to read, very
slowly. He began to read the Bible and use what he had. Our part was
simply to work alongside them and help them understand the scriptural foundations of what God was doing, and God was doing some
wonderful things. I spent time with them, helping them to understand
the Word, but they were doing the evangelism.

I made one bad mistake with Victor Landero though. The first time
I visited his village, he had one little thatched-roof hut, a small planting
of corn, and a few other things. It was hand-to-mouth existence. I was
there for several days and they served me good meals. When I left, I
gave him some money to help cover the expenses of feeding me. That
was a mistake. He accepted my money, but I did not realize at the time
that it was embarrassing to him. It never entered his mind that I should
pay them. Several years later Victor rebuked me, "David, that was a
bad mistake. You never should have paid us. We should have paid you,
because you were the one coming to teach and to help us. The New
Testament says that the laborer is worthy of his hire. We should have
been paying you." That was a wonderful attitude and I appreciated it.

Their evangelism progressed marvelously. I can say without exag-
geration that thousands of people were coming to the Lord in a vast
area, through humble people not connected with the Mission in any
way at all. They never asked for a penny, and we never sent them one.
They were doing their work and are doing it yet. Victor is still out there
way off near the border of Panama in a little Indian tribe where he is
evangelizing. He learned the Indian language on his own by living
among them. He never asked for a penny from anybody. They are
doing it all themselves.

Now a few examples from other parts of the world. When the Friends Missionary Prayer Band was founded years ago, they would not accept money from outside India. They wanted the Indians to pay for their missionaries.

The India Evangelical Mission (the official mission of the Evangelical Fellowship of India, a part of the World Evangelical Fellowship) did the same thing. Established in 1965, their policy was, "We will not accept outside funds. We want Indians to pay for these Indian missionaries who are working cross-culturally within India," and even in other countries.

Finally, Indians living outside India began to say, "Look, you are cutting us off. We want to help our own country. We want to send money."

The mission replied, "No, we don't want your money. We want it to be from India."

And the other people responded, "Yes, but won't you allow us to help because we are Indians too? We just happen to live in another country."

So they finally opened up and said, "Well, okay, for projects, yes. However, we cannot use it for ongoing monthly support of the missionaries. We still have to do that ourselves." So they are doing it and doing it well.

Chuck Bennett of Partners International graciously sent me some correspondence he had recently with Glen Schwartz of World Mission Associates in England. Schwartz takes a strong position on this issue. He believes that no money should go from outside to national workers. Chuck interacted with him, taking a more moderate position. Schwartz quotes an African as saying, "We have now proven that we can raise the money we need within Africa. The biggest problem we now have is the funding which is coming in from the outside, causing problems for us inside."

Chuck responded, "Well, possibly that is true in Kenya, but there are many other places in Africa where that still would not be possible."

Schwartz replied, "I am convinced beyond the shadow of a doubt that Western funding is at the root of the dependence problem. It is among the most important reasons why many mission-established churches do not send out their own missionaries. The availability of Western funds, far from making healthy long-term outreach possible, actually prevents people from believing that they have anything to give to the wider Christian movement unless they are paid by Westerners to do so."

While that may be an extreme viewpoint, it is the feeling of some that Western funds have caused difficulty in not allowing the nationals to have their own vision the way the Friends Missionary Prayer Band and the India Evangelical Mission have done.

Let me mention another experience we had in the Latin America Mission. In 1971 the Latin America Mission decided that the time had come to turn over to the nationals all of the work of the Mission, not just the churches. The local churches had been relinquished years back. However many institutions and ministries were still mission-controlled: a seminary, a radio station, a hospital, a bookstore, and a camp program, among others. It was time to put these into the hands of the nationals, under national leadership. We would work with them and under their leadership, but they had to take over. So we started what was called CLAME, the Spanish acronym, which stands for Latin American Community of Evangelical Ministries. We turned everything over. Every one of those entities established originally by the Mission became independent. We only loan them missionaries, who work under them.

Other missions watched us closely and thought, "You are going quite far on this." They felt that we were getting radical. The Latin America Mission already had somewhat of a radical reputation, and this simply added to it. At the end of ten years, CLAME was dissolved. Some people said, "Well, it failed." No, it did not fail at all. The reason it was dissolved as a structure was because it was no longer needed. Those entities were now independent and conducting their own work.

We ran some risks. We knew that when we turned over the ministries, some might not continue in the track that we hoped they would. That did happen in one classic case. So we would say, "Yes, we lost that one." Parents, when their children become independent, hope that the children will follow the way they have taught them. But they do not always do that.

We took risks in giving them independence and we lost one. But today there are thirty different entities still related in a fraternal way to the Latin America Mission. They are totally autonomous. We only lend them missionaries who work under them. So the plan did work.

I could tell a long story about the Bible Hospital that we had decided to close because we were not making it financially. The Costa Ricans said, "Well, can we run it?" and we said, "If you really want to take it over with full responsibility we will give it to you." We did, and today it is far bigger and more effective than it was under our direction.

Potential Dangers

Finally, let me mention some of the problems that I see and some of the things that worry me. Certain things do bother me. One is the *lumping together of all foreign missionaries as if they are all alike.* I have interacted with K. P. Yohannan on some of his writings. He sent me one of his books and asked my opinion. I wrote a lengthy letter in response and said, "K. P., I think you have been unfair because you have lumped all foreign missionaries together as if they are all the same." For example, he gave the illustration of mass baptisms. That was the Roman Catholic policy during the colonial period of the *Conquistadores.* They would perform mass baptisms on the Indian tribes, and then say that they were all Christians. The implication is that this is the way foreign missionaries work, but national missionaries do not. That is an unfair comparison, because evangelical missionaries have never done that.

Sweeping generalizations say, "All foreign missionaries are like this." But they are not all the same. K. P. gives a tragic example in one of his books of a missionary home where a national visited and sat in the living room. When the national left, the missionary wife got a can of Lysol and sprayed the chair on which he had been sitting. She did not want her chair to be contaminated. The implication is that this is the way foreign missionaries work. While I do not doubt that the story is true, I have never known any missionary among us who would have done such a thing.

Then there is the *either/or* mentality. We do not have any place for that. It is not *either/or.* It's *both/and.* It is not either *colonial* missionaries or *authentic* missionaries. It is *both/and.* We are all part of the Body of Christ. We must work together.

Another thing worries me. When there is too much funding from the States, there is a *lack of accountability locally.* I met a young man in one country who was leading his own work, but who referred to the head of an organization in the States who sent him money as "my boss." This young man was heading his own ministry in his own country, but he saw his boss as an American. This struck me as very unfortunate.

During my years with WEF I traveled to seventy or eighty countries. I repeatedly would find that those who were supported almost exclusively from North America did not relate to the local church well. Their accountability was elsewhere. They felt accountable to the organization in the U. S. that was supporting them. Other nationals would say to me, "So-and-so does not really fit in here. We cannot get him to cooperate because he has accountability outside the country." I have heard some strong complaints. That is one danger of dependency.

Conclusion

In closing let me say three things. First, I read a quotation recently which says, *Don't make the mistake of feeling that you have to tear down one thing in order to promote another.* If we tear down another way of mission so that we can promote our way of doing it, that is not right.

Second, when I came back to the U. S. to work with Inter-Varsity, I landed among university students in the late '60s and early '70s. That was the era of the counter culture movement among students. Talk about culture shock! I had far more culture shock then than I had ever had when I first went to Latin America. That generation was rebelling and raising all kinds of trouble. Students were negative about missions. Since I am a missionary, they would talk to me about colonialism and paternalism, asserting that missionaries have always been wrong. I had a terrible time getting students to face their biblical responsibility.

I finally found a method that worked. I would say to the students, "Okay, let us suppose for the sake of discussion that every missionary who ever served in foreign missions was a 100 percent failure. Everything they did was wrong. Everything was colonialistic. Everything was paternalistic. Right? Let's accept that for a moment. What does that have to do with *your responsibility*—your response to the Great Commission, when God tells *you* that you are responsible to get the gospel to the whole world?" Now I would apply that reasoning here. Even if all foreign missions had been totally wrong from day one, how do I respond to God when He tells me that I am to take the gospel to those who have never heard? Do I just send money, or do I incarnate myself among them?

I go back to my experience in Colombia. How could I have helped Victor Landero and those people by sending money? They did not need my money. I could help them only by incarnating myself with them and by helping them to understand the Scriptures. If I had not gone, if I had simply sent them money, they would not have been taught. They needed an incarnational presence—the help of someone right there with them. I was responding personally to God's Great Commission to be part of what He was doing.

The hand can never say to the eye, "I do not need you." The task of world evangelization is far too big for any one segment of the Church to do it alone. We need each other.

CHAPTER 5

What Have We Learned?

John C. Bennett

The danger in trying to answer "What have we learned?" for a consultation is that we will be satisfied with an account of what new information or ideas have been placed on the table, and shy away from a discriminating critique and reflection. This is a frequent pattern with respect to events, to judge one as successful because there was good attendance and an abundance of material was delivered. Indeed, my initial assignment was to edit a transcript of the final morning's session, comprised of reports from various small groups. For good or for ill, I have elected not to pursue this course. What I attempt here is to answer the "So what?" question.

In 1975 I served an innovative Christian ministry that endeavored (and still endeavors today) to help local churches understand the global implications of Christian faith for their lives and ministries. We were working on a seminar to help church leaders grapple with the "purposes" for their ministries of international and cross-cultural impact. It is never easy to stimulate people to take time to consider something as apparently mundane as a purpose statement. Part of the problem is in the very word "purpose." "Let's not worry about this," many would say. "Let's just get on with it."

One day in the midst of this design exercise I had lunch with Ed Dayton, who was then the Director of the Missions Advanced Research and Communications division of World Vision International. Ed was very influential on me in terms of how to think about the future. He introduced to me the notion that goals are "statements of faith." Perhaps even more important, he taught me that a purpose statement is a way of describing *how the world will be different because of who you are and what you do*. It is under this rubric that I would like to reflect on the first Consultation on the Support of Indigenous Ministries. So what? How might the world be different because we met for three and a half days in Wheaton in October 1996?

The most profound outcome of this Consultation was the demonstration of a movement in formation. I remember when Chuck

Bennett of Partners International called me in 1995 to see if Overseas Council would be willing to back a one-off event to bring together North American ministries uniquely focused on enabling indigenous ministries in the non-Western world. My first response to Chuck, and probably a skeptical one, had to do with the viability of the idea. Were there enough such ministries, and would the will to gather be concrete? We had worked fairly closely with PI over the years because of our common interests in leadership development and theological education, but I was rather unaware of the other "players," apart from a few names such as Christian Aid Mission and Gospel for Asia. My impression was that few of these organizations were "mainstreamed" into the broader missions community, with the exception of PI, and that most were rather independent-minded and self-sufficient. It takes at least two to dance, and I wondered in my own mind if a *consultation* in the true sense of the word would be of interest. In fairness, Overseas Council has been better connected with Two-Thirds World training networks and churches, and we simply did not know the indigenous ministries scene in North America.

Chuck then began to unwind some of his conversations with what I later discovered from Dan Rickett are as many as one hundred or more ministries based in North America that are exclusively focused on enabling and partnering with indigenous ministries. Moreover, Chuck had already secured the support of Christian Aid Mission, Gospel for Asia, Ambassadors for Christ, and others to form a planning committee for the event, and had sounded a dozen or so other organizations in terms of participation. This began to appear promising. The short story is that the Consultation attracted more than 100 representatives from 52 agencies, which was right on target with Chuck's projections. He may remember my occasional questions in the run-up to the event that subtly (or perhaps not so subtly!) continued to ask about the viability of the idea. I was proven wrong.

However, it was not participation or representation that demonstrated an emerging movement. To my way of thinking, a movement is more than simply a network of people or organizations with common interests. You have to add passion to a network in order to achieve a movement, and there has to be a growing sense of interdependence. In addition one needs to see a willingness to refine and even modify organizational priorities and approaches in order to collectively achieve a common mission or purpose. It's more than simply a professional association. I like the analogy of a trade union through which workers in a common profession not only talk shop, compare notes, and sharpen their skills, but they also organize to accomplish something collectively that is perhaps unachievable without collaboration.

The elements of an emerging movement were there at Wheaton in October 1996. We had passion. One of the highlights of the event was the banquet held in honor of our movement's pioneers. Bob Finley is a controversial fellow. He admits it. But here is a man who recognized three decades ago that the center of gravity of the global Christian movement had shifted to the South and that the future of world evangelization lay in the hands of non-Western Christian workers. Bob has persevered in that vision because of his passion, and it is contagious.

During the Consultation I had a friendly and private conversation with Allen Finley, Bob's brother and another person who has been very influential on my thinking regarding organizational leadership and particularly the connection between senior leadership, vision casting, and resource development. Allen told me some of his experiences in trying to connect PI (then Christian Nationals Evangelism Commission) with the more traditional mission agency community in North America. His early experiences at various association meetings in those camps were not terribly welcoming. But he stuck it out. Because of his passion. Today the cause of support and partnership with indigenous ministries is a core concern for every credible mission sending agency that I know, and people like Allen have cast vision for that cause in their midst. This is a mark of passion.

But I found passion for the cause throughout the spectrum of participants. This was not always reflected only in what people came to say or to communicate, but was also evident in their intense desire to be better equipped to carry out the ministries to which they believe the Lord has called them. This is a biblical pattern—to be learners, to be teachable, and to recognize when there is wisdom to be gained. This was a spiritually mature group comprised of people who did not come to "lead," but to learn to be better servants. I believe that this is a more reliable measure of passion for a cause than any degree of urgency to seek recognition or leadership.

There was a surprising (at least to me) transparency within the group, especially for a gathering of people who were mainly meeting each other for the first time. The two devotional studies and biblical reflections that K. P. Yohannan gave us were characteristic of this trait. All of us could identify with K. P.'s declaration and illustrations that ministry is a battle. The fact is, the organizations represented at the Consultation are often misunderstood, criticized for fostering unhealthy dependencies, and accused of somehow being "anti-mission." Later in this reflection I want to come back to the need for this movement to examine itself with regard to those critiques, and to respond cogently. But it was clear that many in the room were identifying with the pain that K. P. and his colleagues have suffered through opposition of varying sorts, not just "on the field" but North America, as well. I know that I appreciated his candor and willingness to be open about such struggles.

One of the legitimate critiques of the 1996 Consultation was that we had a rather large share of platform time given to comments and presentations by those whose ministries are in a strict sense a step removed from the support of indigenous ministries. Incidentally, I will agree that the critique is valid, and those of us who served on the planning committee knew ahead of time that this criticism would arise. This is the difficulty of emerging movements and their initial gatherings. It is difficult to secure a program team until you have had some experience to work with.

Nevertheless, this weakness in design also revealed the willingness of participants to hear out constructive criticisms of the movement. This is not to say that any of the program personnel came as detractors. But the willingness of the Consultation to hear outside voices allowed some key issues to be raised. These included the suitability of the term "indigenous" to describe what we do in a positive light from the non-Western standpoint. (Indeed, even as I write, the term "non-Western" has its difficulties.) We were asked, "Who is serving whom?" This is an essential question when we deal with ministries that develop resources for others which are at the same time the means of supply for the serving organization.

We were challenged to recognize the contributions of more traditional mission organizations and to seek ways to collaborate with them. We were reminded by one speaker that, "There are fraudulent schemes in our movement." Promotion using "more bang for the buck" lingo was questioned as to its truthfulness and its appropriateness. We were called to break down competitive patterns and speak well of one another in private. And the notion that the West is the chief source of financial resources was challenged and rejected. These are tough themes for an emerging movement to deal with. Indeed, we did not deal with all of them (or perhaps any of them) in finality. But I was impressed that the participants "from the movement" were willing to hear these critiques, and in turn constructively criticize the event for not providing sufficient time for members of the movement to speak to each other in response to them. An aside, the successor consultation in 1997 is being designed to yield just such an opportunity.

But an emerging movement does not simply arise from passion, whether that passion yields the desire to grow in knowledge, wisdom, and competence, or to be willing to hear criticism that is constructively offered. An emerging movement must also reflect on that passion and yield a cohesive vision for the future. On two occasions, one more briefly and another at length on the closing morning, we had the opportunity for plenary discussion along the lines of "What are we hearing and saying?" This is a natural challenge for ministries that have learned to function—of necessity—in very independent ways. How do you transform a group of independent contractors into a cohesive trade union or movement? I shared the following anecdote with the Consultation as an illustration of the problem.

In 1970 I landed my first full-time job. During the summer months of that year I worked for the Atlantic Richfield Company in California in a public relations exercise to alert drivers to the extent of air pollution produced by automobiles. We operated a roving emission testing center throughout Southern California. For the month of August I had to commute weekly from my home in Los Angeles to the work site in San Diego. At that time the California Department of Transportation was constructing the interchange between Interstate 5 and Interstate 8, fairly close to downtown San Diego. It was the state's largest interchange project at the time. As you traveled south on I-5 and came down out of the La Jolla hills, you could see it in the distance. As one got closer, the structure became larger, and then you could see what was wrong with it. Here were multiple levels of concrete ramps going off into thin air, connected to nothing. And it had been that way for about two years. Something was clearly wrong. The construction workers, who were legion and working feverishly every day, had painted a sign for motorists to see. It said: "WE DON'T KNOW WHAT IT IS—WE ARE JUST TRYING TO BUILD IT."

In many respects the population of ministries committed to the support of indigenous ministries are subject to the same critique. We are busy. Very busy. And in many cases over-busy. We are each trying to respond to our understanding of a vision for partnering with and enabling the church in the Two-Thirds World as they emerge as full partners in the global Christian movement. What we have sensed is that an ad hoc approach to building our network will not do. We want to know and understand what we are building.

The Consultation made both implicit and explicit calls for the formation of a radical fellowship of ministries. I use the term "radical" in the sense of *foundational* and *fundamental*. We will be building from the ground up, and our needs reflect this. As a movement of organizations we need to know one another. Not "know" in the promotional sense, but in a real sense. The kind of knowing that allows for biblical principles of corporate rejoicing and suffering to be applied. We need true fellowship mechanisms to be put into place.

In addition to relational underpinnings, this movement and its members need to be "reading on the same page." This means shared values, shared definitions, and shared standards of action and performance. Furthermore, we need to recognize that in advocating partnership and support of indigenous ministries we are endeavoring to place a twentieth/twenty-first century paradigm for ministry in some contrast with a nineteenth century model. By this we do not mean that mission sending from the West is passé. What has been superseded is the notion that the progress of the Gospel, the Kingdom, and world evangelization is exclusively or even primarily dependent upon Western hands. This movement is a statement of recognition of and commitment to this overarching value and reality.

Having said this, some at the Consultation (and I would echo this concern) asked if we can go forward without integral linkages to the denominational and interdenominational missionary-sending structures in the Western context. I think that the answer is decidedly negative. Not only would this be unbiblical in that it works against the unity of the Body of Christ in ministry, but also there are practical reasons that our movement cannot remain independent of the more traditional mission organizations. The Two-Thirds World is a very denominational place. The independent or non-denominational church movements that are quite pronounced in the West, and out of which much of our movement arises, is not as much of a reality or future prospect in the non-Western world. Indeed, it has been denominations, many of them with linkages to expatriate mission organizations, that have built the very infrastructures being supported by our movement. This is not to say that independent church movements do not exist in the Two-Thirds World, but they are not a majority and in many places not even a large minority.

Similarly, we also touched on whether or not we can take forward a movement such as ours without the presence and active participation of those from Africa, Asia, Latin America, and East Central Europe who represent the ministries with which we are linked. The very fact that the work of our movement is not focused on the West suggests that those from the Two-Thirds World should be a part of us, not merely for fellowship, but also for strategic thinking, planning, and consensus decision-making. Our initial gathering did not significantly facilitate such participation, and I am unsure that the successor event will do so because the implementation of this value has not been sufficiently in view.

In trying to answer the "So what?" question, it is also helpful to recollect the values affirmed by the Consultation in the course of its deliberations. What was suggested as important for us? Servanthood was stressed by many, indicating that the *end* of our ministries must not be their own perpetuation. At the same time, a premium was placed on perseverance in the face of opposition, whether from so-called "resistant countries" or the unsubstantiated criticisms of the support of indigenous ministries. We placed value on the need to be vision casters; i.e., people and ministries who can articulate biblical vision in a compelling way and thus strengthen our organizations. Related to the casting of vision is its development through networking and collaboration, as opposed to the model of independency that says, "The Lord is leading us. I hope He is leading you as well. Good luck."

We stressed the need for the development of sufficient and capable leaders within our own ministries. We stressed the need for the internationalization of material support for indigenous ministries, including the development of resources locally and breaking down the myths that increasing self-reliance in the Two-Thirds World is impossible. We affirmed that in a spiritual sense we need to seek to please the Lord and that faith in action yields precisely this result. And as cautionary values, we were reminded that there is a tendency today for relationships to be subordinated to strategy, and that ministries which were at one time focused on spiritual transformation have become obsessed with spiritual transactions. These warnings against adverse values were also part of our Consultation experience.

I mentioned earlier the danger in evaluating an event simply in terms of attendance and the delivery of information. But even the reflective outcomes of a consultation can be deceptive in value. The first time that a group gets around a subject, it is easy to think that we understand the whole, that we have a clear view of the past and a valid vision for the future. Certainly, we made progress in these directions, but we ought to take warning from the anecdote that is often told in the southern cone of South America.

A freighter was caught between the Argentine and the British navies during the Falklands War, or the Malvinas War if you take it from the Argentine perspective. The freighter captain was under orders to sail a course that would take them between the two navies. Unfortunately, the armadas had declared an exclusion zone. Anything sailing in this zone would be blown out of the water. Suddenly the captain got a brilliant idea. He organized his crew to paint the starboard side of the ship blue and white, being the colors of the Argentine flag. On the port side of the ship he painted the Union Jack. As he sailed between the two navies he could hear the Argentines on the right screaming, "Viva! Viva! Viva!" He could also hear the British on the left side saying, "Hip Hip Hooray! Hip Hip Hooray!" Reaching the end of the gauntlet, the captain was thrilled with his success, so he said to his crew, "That was tremendous! Let's turn around and do it again."

Like the freighter captain, our movement runs the risk of triumphal ignorance, a failure to comprehend reality in the midst of apparent progress and success. Indeed, we have made progress. A movement is emerging. This is a union of organizations that shares passion for the cause of the support of indigenous ministries. There is compelling need and opportunity to build bridges of partnership between the West and the ministries in the Majority World. We are on the right track. But there are number of potential pitfalls. If we are not self critical in a constructive sense then we run the risk of simply turning the ship around, doing it again, and finding out that we have ignored the areas in which we must improve in order to accomplish our God-given purposes.

Key challenges to our movement and issues that we must address, especially in the second consultation scheduled for September 1997, include the following. We must deal constructively with the critique that the financial support of indigenous ministries fosters dependency more than self-reliance. It is not difficult to answer the objection that material resources should never be shared internationally or among material unequals. The II Corinthian texts regarding the Pauline collection (chapter 8 for example) establish the validity of international financial partnerships for ministry outcomes.

The deeper question is whether we are prosecuting our model for ministry in a way that truly seeks for and enables increasing self-reliance among indigenous ministries. This takes us back to models for partnership, and whether we function primarily as *relief organizations* that meet needs, or as *developmental organizations* that catalyze and build capacity. Related to this, we must also look at the nature of partnership and ask whether our two-dimensional thinking (i.e., bilateral partnerships) is sufficient. This also returns us to the matter of multilateral relationships that might include church structures as well as more traditional mission structures and sending organizations.

We must also look at how our movement grows and promotes itself. Every industry has its frauds and shady operators. Ours is no exception. Fortunately, our consultations and the way they are structured tend to bring out only those who are rightly motivated and prepared to be accountable. At the same time, even ministries that are committed to legitimacy can be tempted to use means and methods of communication that are deceptive. Estimates of results can be inflated simply by the interpretation of reporting data by many different people in our organizations.

As mentioned previously, many of us subtly—or perhaps not so subtly—use the "more bang for the buck" rationale in seeking donor investments. Is this a right value? It becomes an even more complex issue when we realize that this value is strongly held by many major donors and partners whose ability to contribute significantly to our ministries arise from their very strong work ethics. Do our partners in the Majority World know what we are saying about them and their ministries? If not, what would they think and what would they feel if they did know and understand the nature of our promotional language? These are questions and issues which we must not leave to those outside of our movement to ask. Perhaps a way forward is to develop a code of ethics or other standards of practice that we voluntarily and corporately affirm and account for to one another.

We must also look at the degree of competition that exists within our movement and among the organizations that comprise it. Personally, I do not struggle greatly with the principle of competition per se. Scripture speaks of a group of men "sharpening" one another. This is very much a competitive image. It is applicable not merely to men, but to all individual Christians who wish to grow in excellence. We can also apply this to groups of ministries that wish to grow in excellence together, and I hope this includes our movement. At the same time, I believe that we need to be more concerned with how we cooperate and collaborate with each other *in practical, concrete terms*, than how well we compete with one another.

Multilateral resourcing of projects.

Sharing of human resources and expertise.

Joint proposals to funding consortia and foundations.

Coordination of relationships and investments by similar ministries in common geographical or cultural contexts.

Sharing of evaluative information on project activities, within the limits of confidentiality.

These are some of the potential pieces of the mosaic of collaboration that could mark our movement. Will we structure our fellowship, perhaps as a formal association, in a way that creates time and space for designing and implementing this kind of cooperation?

These are the questions which are in my mind as we look toward gathering again in September this year. Because of my personal involvement in the planning committee for the 1997 Consultation, I can say that we have considered these questions and others in the design of the event. But it will be left to all of us who participate later this year to determine whether good intentions and good planning yield a productive reality. I was asked by a member of the media whether our 1996 consultation was in any sense a defining moment for our movement and, perhaps, for the wider Church. My answer was affirmative because of the nature of a first-time event. Last year's consultation was a milestone. Whether our 1997 gathering will be a true turning point or watershed for Kingdom ministry as we move into the twenty-first century still remains to be seen. By God's grace, may it be so.

CHAPTER 6

Pauline Patterns of Church-Mission Relationships

George W. Peters

Observations have frequently been made that the Bible does not prescribe specific patterns of relationship between mission agencies and national churches. Such relationships seem to be open to history, circumstances, and human wisdom. However, such statements must be accepted with caution. They must not be interpreted to mean that the Bible does not offer decisive, abiding guiding principles. It seems reasonable to expect that the Lord of missions and the churches would not leave the people of God without guidance in such important matters. Neither is Paul, the master builder, silent on this issue.

Our problem is not the lack of revealed guiding principles. Rather, several blindfolds seem to obscure our ability to comprehend them. First, the church-mission relationship on the home base has become seriously blurred. It is not biblically defined or clearly understood. A serious dichotomy between churches and mission societies has developed. Therefore, we have many missionless churches and many church-less mission societies. Because of this non-relationship between many churches and mission societies on the home base, the relationship on the field is not fully understood and it suffers accordingly. The abnormality of the home situation carries over to the field. It reflects itself in abnormalities and tensions in the new situation.

Second, the underlying issues of the mission-church problem are not fully grasped and dealt with in concrete, realistic terms. Ideologies, sentiments, tradition, nationalism (in the missions and in the churches), immaturity, inflexibility, organizational identity and/or organizational dominance are all involved. Not least is a peculiar concept of the indigeneity of the church that many a missionary carries with him and seeks to practice. It is difficult to penetrate to the core and define the real issues of mission-church tensions. It must also be recognized that the concerns differ with missions, churches, peoples, and times. Denominational missions do not face the same problems as do interdenominational missions. The problems in former colonial areas are not the same as they are in countries that have not gone through this experience. Tribal churches differ greatly from city churches.

Third, great variations exist in mission and church organizations, background, training, home church relationships, and theological concepts. The different early practices in the fields by different missions and missionaries and the isolationist mentality of numerous missionaries create difficulties in recognizing guiding principles laid down in Scripture. These blindfolds constitute formidable obstacles to the work of the Holy Spirit. Only a divine breakthrough among the missions and the churches can lead us through the maze. In this situation let us look at Paul and learn some guiding principles from him.

Paul speaks of himself as a master builder (1 Cor. 3:10). We recognize Paul's missionary principles as divine revelation, and therefore normative for all times. It is important, however, to distinguish his principles from his missionary practices and patterns. The latter are not necessarily normative for all times and all people. His practices and patterns are culturally related and are therefore relative. Paul was creative, flexible, and adaptable. He was sensitive to people and their culture (1 Cor. 9:19–23). There is both the constant and the adaptable in Paul. He never changed his message, goals, and principles, but he did change his approaches, methods, practices, and patterns. Most certainly mission-church relationships are involved in missionary principles. We therefore have a right to look at Paul and the Scriptures for guidance.

Pauline Missionary-Church Relationships

Paul expresses his missionary-church relationship in a brief but meaningful phrase: "Your fellowship (koinonia) in the gospel from the first day until now" (Phil. 1:5). A closely related passage is found in Romans 15:24, where Paul expresses the expectation that the church in Rome will help him on his way to Spain. The key word is koinonia. Thayer translates it as: fellowship, association, community, communion, joint participation, intercourse. Vine adds: partnership, partner, partaker, fellowship, communion, contribution. Bensler takes it to mean: *gemeinschaft, anteil, teilahme, verbindung, vereinigung, umgang.* William Barkley speaks of it as a sharing of friendship, practical sharing with those less fortunate, partnership in the work of Christ.

Paul uses the word koinonia four times in Philippians: fellowship in the gospel (1:5), fellowship in the Spirit (2:1), fellowship in his sufferings (3:10), fellowship of my affliction (4:14). In 4:14 a related word is used to express the fact of financial sharing in his life and ministry.

However we may interpret the working methods and practices of Paul, his missionary-church relationship principle is clear. It is a relationship of partnership in the full sense of the word. His relationship would not fit into the modern patterns of parallelism or of merger. Paul never thought of himself as separate from the churches he founded. Spiritual, theological, cultural, ecclesiastical, or organizational dichotomy would have seemed strange to Paul and totally unacceptable to him. He was too closely related to and too intimately bound up in the life of the churches. But Paul was not so completely merged with the churches and submerged in church ministries that his divine calling and commission as a missionary to the nations were imperiled. Phillips translates Romans 15:23: "But now, since my work in these places no longer needs my presence..." Paul felt his time had come to move on. The apostle avoided both extremes. Neither dichotomy (parallelism) nor merger would have fitted this pattern. He labored in partnership with the churches.

Paul's partnership relationship was one of full participation in the life of the churches—in their mobilization and enlistment of prayer, personnel, and finances. Paul found the resources for all his advances in evangelism and church expansion in the churches he had planted. The churches became involved with Paul from the very beginning in an aggressive program of evangelism and church multiplication. This is evident from such church reports of gospel outreach as Luke records in Acts 13:49; 19:10, 20, 26.

Such reports could not have been written had Paul operated as a mission society apart from the churches. Neither could Paul have written that he had fully preached the gospel from Jerusalem to Illyricum (modern Yugoslavia), had he not fully mobilized the churches in partnership in evangelism (Rom. 15:19). It is also evident that the churches remained in such partnership throughout the apostle's life. It never became a question which ministries and projects belonged to the mission and which to the churches. Theirs was a total partnership ministry from the very beginning. No transfer ever became necessary.

Pauline Principles

Several guiding principles evolve from Philippians 1:5 and the rest of the epistle. Partnership included the free sharing of all resources for the proclamation of the gospel and the evangelization of the communities. Paul's finances all came from the mission fields (Phil. 2:25; 4:15; Rom. 15:24). The New English Bible translates the latter passage: "for I hope to see you as I travel through, and to be sent there (Spain) with your support after having enjoyed your company for a while." All of Paul's associates came from the churches he founded, and it can be assumed that they were sustained by the churches. Most probably they were all or mostly Paul's own converts. The only exception may be Silas, the Silvanus of the epistles, who joined Paul in Jerusalem. However, Silas, too, was a Roman citizen (Acts 16:37).

Partnership was natural because it was introduced from the very beginning of the ministries. Evangelism was caught by the churches as much as it was taught to them. Paul was not working for them but rather with them. From the very beginning the churches were schools of practical evangelism. Partnership continued throughout the lifetime of the apostle. Paul remained related to the churches and their care was upon him continuously (cf. Phil. 4:18; I Cor. 11:18.)

Partnership excluded the lording of one party over the other. Never did Paul demand or legislate the partnership of the churches. He solicited and elicited partnership in missions. Paul's attitude in partnership in missions must not be confused with his authoritative pronouncements in doctrine, his legislation in moral matters, and his discipline in moral and doctrinal matters. Such authority was his because of his divine calling to the apostleship. He did not exercise such authority in missionary partnership in that he was a humble brother and energetic leader among fellow-laborers, and a dynamic and exemplary force in the churches in evangelism and church expansion.

Partnership relationship in missions between Paul and the churches grew out of deeper levels of fellowship—fellowship in the Spirit, fellowship in the sufferings, fellowship in the apostle's afflictions. Paul's complete identification with the churches in love, life, and ministries made fellowship on the deepest level possible and resulted in a natural partnership in missions. It would have seemed strange practice to Paul to find in a common field of labor a "fellowship of the mission" and a "fellowship of the national churches." Such dichotomy Paul could have never tolerated, no matter how well-meant and how ideally defended.

Partnership in missions excluded the demand of the churches for complete merger of the missionaries with the churches and the subservience of one party to the other. The common goal of world evangelism forbade the capturing of the mission and missionaries by the churches. Outreach, not inreach, was the dominant note and thrust. Partnership meant the "let go" (Acts 13:3) of the workers as well as cooperation in the laborers.

Pauline Premises

Such partnership relationship rested, however, upon specific premises which are evident from the book of Acts and the Pauline epistles. Paul recognized the churches as duly constituted churches of Jesus Christ from the very beginning. He respected them as churches and expected them to function as the church of God in their specific communities. There came a time for the missionary (and the mission) to move on (Rom. 15:15–24).

Paul recognized the gifts of the Holy Spirit and believed that the Holy Spirit would enable and qualify every constituted church to function adequately without the importation of special help from the outside. Temporary teaching and organizing help may be wise and some follow-up ministry is required. However, Paul expected the churches to function under the Lordship of Christ and the direction of the Holy Spirit as self-sufficient units.

Paul was less concerned about establishing autonomous and indigenous churches. These were peripheral concepts. He labored strenuously and incessantly to establish truly Christian and evangelizing churches. In this he was remarkably successful, as the seven churches around Ephesus and the evangelizing efforts of the church in Thessalonica show.

Paul's view of service and missionary partnership is wholly positive. Service in the New Testament is as much a divine means of Christian growth as it is the result of Christian maturity. Missions is not an optional enterprise, it is the life-flow of the church. Missionary partnership must be built into the church from the very beginning. Without it no church will reach its full maturity. Service is not only for the perfect, it is a means for the perfecting of the saints.

Paul depended upon the gospel of the universal love of God, the greatness of the work of Christ, and the abiding presence of the Holy Spirit to motivate and direct the churches in their gospel partnership. Paul expected that his own example would set the evangelizing pattern for the churches and lead them on in their evangelistic outreach and missionary partnership. Unhesitatingly, he called upon the churches to follow him as he was following Christ (1 Cor. 4:16; 11:1; 1 Thess. 1:6).

In these days of tensions, gropings, and searchings for answers to the problems of mission-church relationship, we would do well to look more closely and confidently to the Apostle Paul as an example and to the Holy Spirit to show us some of his guiding principles of partnership in missions. We will not find it easy to enter into true partnership. Partnership eliminates the over-against, the side-by-side, the one-over-the-other, and the one submerging in the other.

Partnership in missions means equals are bound together in mutual confidence, unified purpose, and united effort. They accept equal responsibilities, authority, praise, and blame; they share burdens, joys, sorrows, victories, and defeats. Partnership means joint planning, joint legislation, and joint programming. Sending and receiving churches are on an equal basis. Only the closest bond in Christ enriched by humility, love, confidence, and self-giving will actualize partnership. Partnership in missions is as much an attitude, a spiritual, social and theological relationship, a philosophy of ministry, and a way of life, as it is a defined pattern of church-mission relationship for administration and legislation.

I am not blind to the fact that the transition from the Pauline world and mission to our time, situation, and ministry is not easily made. The mission world and circumstances of Paul differed greatly from our mission world. The dominant Hellenism, cross-cultural fertilization, economic prosperity, relative safety, philosophical bankruptcy, cross-racial movements, and religious ferment constituted unique circumstances for the flow and reception of the gospel of Jesus Christ. Only a few of these factors are making themselves felt in our modern days.

Paul was a citizen of the world in which he labored and not a guest in a foreign country, as most missionaries are. He enjoyed the hospitality of a government under specific conditions. The apostle had no language to learn. He was born in a mission field and had no cultural barriers to overcome. Monotheism was widespread and much respected. Old Testament ethical principles had been widely advocated by Jewish writers. Most of Paul's churches were founded in cities where Jews, proselytes, and godfearers constituted a goodly portion of the people. Seldom did Paul come to communities where he did not have some previous contacts. He was therefore able to find accommodation and begin his ministry with some friends or acquaintances.

Paul had tremendous advantages from many points of view. From a practical point of comparison, Paul operated in a home mission field. It is therefore difficult to carry over Paul's methods, practices, and patterns in totality and without qualifications into our situation and into our times. We must make allowances for many variables. The idea that we can "do as Paul did it" may betray more naivete than wisdom, more idealism than realism. We must remain sober and balanced.

The fact remains, however, that the principle of partnership is not affected by these variables. The principles of partnership do not rest in culture, times, or circumstances. Partnership is a relationship rooted in the mission's identification with the churches on the deepest levels of fellowship in the Spirit, and in mutual burdens, interests, purposes, and goals. Partnership is not circumstantial, it is a matter of life, health, and relationship. It belongs to the nature of Christianity. It is not optional, it is bound up in Christian fellowship and progress.

Although the working out of the principle of partnership may take on different patterns, the patterns will be determined by the principle. The patterns cannot conflict with the principle. There must be formal and functional harmony and symmetry between the outer and the inner, the body and the spirit. Somehow the patterns must portray partnership.

The principle of partnership is comprehensive. It determines programming, planning, financing, and personnel appointment and assignment as these factors relate to the mission's outreach, and as they involve the missions and the churches in the task of evangelism and other mutually agreed upon projects. In all things it behooves us to keep the unity of the Spirit in the bond of peace and to demonstrate our mutuality and equality in Christ and in his cause before the world.

CHAPTER 7

Towards True Mutuality
Exchanging the Same Commodities or Supplementing Each Others' Needs?

David J. Bosch

My purpose is to examine the whole area of the relationships between "older" and "younger" churches with a particular focus on the so-called moratorium issue. I am aware that the moratorium call has, by and large, been sounded only in those Third World churches affiliated with the World Council of Churches; in Roman Catholic and conservative-evangelical churches, moratorium does not appear to be so much an issue. However, I am concerned about the whole issue of true mutuality—something in which we should all be vitally interested, completely apart from the question of whether moratorium will not yet become an issue in other churches as well.

The moratorium cry has so far been heard almost exclusively in those younger churches established quite a while ago; mostly in the previous century. The majority of the younger churches that have come into existence as a result of evangelical missions are, however, much more recent in origin. They have therefore perhaps simply not yet reached the stage where they feel the presence of the Western church and missionary organizations as an unbearable burden. But there is no guarantee that such a stage will not come.

In this study we will first look, very briefly, at the development of the idea of mutual relationships in this century. Next, we will note that in spite of everything that was achieved, the moratorium issue arose. Then we will try to analyze the true reasons for the moratorium demand. And lastly, we will seek to identify some elements of true mutuality as a possible way out of the present dilemma.

Development of Mutual Relationships

In discussing the development of mutual relationships, I will take as my point of orientation the various international missionary conferences—simply because in such conferences one finds a crystallizing of issues as well as an element of representativeness that are not easily detectable elsewhere. For example, in the Roman Catholic Church the whole issue of relationships between the "old" and the "young" church surfaced much later than in the Protestant churches for a great variety of reasons. One of these is to be found in the fact that the Roman Catholic Church used to have an extremely centralized understanding of the Church. In fact, it would not be entirely wrong to argue that the "local church" was only "discovered" during Vatican II and that, since then, there has been a much greater emphasis on decentralization or, rather, localization. But this has, at the same time, created the possibility for a moratorium call in the Roman Catholic Church as well.

During the Edinburgh Conference (1910) the issue of relationships between older and younger churches was hardly touched upon. The younger churches were at best "missionary media" who did not act on their own but only insofar as they were assisted by Western missionary bodies—and this in spite of the fact that Henry Venn and Rufus Anderson had propagated the "three selves" almost sixty years earlier. The whole issue was under the surface, however, and did surface clearly at least once: in the paper read by the young Indian, V. S. Azariah, who lauded the missionaries for everything they had done and given, but then challenged them with the words, "Give us friends!"

When the Jerusalem conference assembled 18 years later, the situation was markedly different. Not only were the younger churches now much better represented, but also the terminology betrayed the dawning of a new era. There were frequent references to "partnership," "equality," "cooperation," "community," "mutual relationships" and "solidarity." Jerusalem went on to judge that the time was ripe for the younger churches to be invited to send missionaries with special commissions to the West.

The Tambaram conference of 1938 added little to our subject. Tambaram's preoccupation lay elsewhere, namely the relationship to non-Christian religions.

When the first post-war meeting of the International Missionary Council gathered in Whitby, Ontario, in 1947, it was immediately evident that a completely new situation had developed, and that it would never again be possible to return to the non-committal talk that marked much of the pre-war discussion of mutual relationships. Real progress was made at Whitby. It is important to note, however, that the progress was not in the first place to be ascribed to profounder theological insights, but rather to events in world history. Many younger churches had been made independent rather violently by the circumstances of the war when all communications with their respective supporting agencies in the West were cut off, and they were not prepared to revert to their pre-war relationships as if nothing had happened. This was all the more the case as a number of Third World countries now found themselves on the road to political independence, and their churches were not willing to be found lagging behind. So new relationships were very much needed and Whitby gave expression to its support for these by coining the phrase "partnership in obedience."

Whitby exuded a spirit of optimism. Much was also expected of the new formula. When the IMC met again five years later in Willingen, Germany, the atmosphere was different. Great uncertainty prevailed. The shadow of the "missionary debacle in China" hung over the conference. It was already clear that the world would never again revert to the equilibrium of the period before World War II. It was also becoming evident that "partnership in obedience" was no magic formula and operated with difficulty, despite goodwill on both sides. The partnership idea was broadly discussed and an emphasis was laid on "mission in unity."

The last general conference of the IMC took place in Ghana, 1958, but no new magical slogan was concocted there. Signs of the impatience of the younger churches with Western churches and missionary societies surfaced, and the cry, "missionary, go home!" was heard, although not as shrilly as later. A very perceptive Dutch mission board secretary, Count van Randwijck, remarked in his report:

Unless missions catch a new vision of their task, the days of their partnership and cooperation in the lands of their present-day activity will be numbered, even if they keep alive for quite a considerable time. We must not let their still intact position in some parts of the world and the useful things they are doing everywhere allow us to dodge this issue (1958:99).

Subsequent international meetings, now of the Commission on World Mission and Evangelism of the World Council of Churches, experimented with other formulas. The Mexico City meeting of 1963 coined the formula JAM, "Joint Action for Mission," which remained in vogue for some time. The Uppsala meeting of the WCC (1968) spoke of "multilateral relations;" at the request of the assembly a portfolio for "Ecumenical Sharing of Personnel" (ESP) was called into being. Bangkok (1973) came to light with "mature relationships."

A few words should be said about the development of multilateral relationships. Whitby's formula, "partnership in obedience," was basically aimed at bilateral relationships and this is where part of the

problem lay. Such a bilateral relationship meant for instance, a relationship between the Lutheran Church in Germany and the Lutheran
Church in Tanzania which came into being through the mission work
of the former. But because of the inherited relationships of dominance
and dependence which had become fossilized in the course of years,
such a partnership tended to be locked almost completely into paternalistic categories. Thus bilateral relationships were often "power
relationships" of the strong with the weak. As an Indonesian church
leader trenchantly expressed it to a Dutch delegation: "The partnership for you; the obedience for us."

So the attempt was made to create multilateral ties between
churches not necessarily burdened with hereditary overtones of paternalism. Thus the base was considerably broadened. A number of those
relationships came into existence, such as the Communauté Evangélique
d'Action Apostolique, which established structural ties between 23
churches in 12 countries. Similar multilateral structures were set up
between churches on the European continent and in Indonesia, as well
as between several American and Japanese churches. The Bangkok
conference of 1973 also urged a fundamental revision of bilateral
structures and relationships.

The Call for Moratorium

When Bangkok met, it was, however, already two years after John
Gatu of Kenya, in a paper read in New York, suggested a moratorium
of five years on Western missionary involvement in Africa. Here he still
used the word "moratorium" in its original meaning of "deferment for
a limited period." A few months later, however, addressing a meeting
of the Reformed Church in America in Milwaukee, he changed that to
"Missionaries should be withdrawn. Period."

On the other side of the Pacific in Kuala Lampur, Emerito Nacpil
of the Philippines was saying essentially the same thing at the same
time: "…the most missionary service a missionary under the present
system can do today for Asia is to go home! And the most free and vital
and daring act the younger churches can do today is to stop asking for
missionaries under the present system" (n.d.:78–79). Paul Verghese
from India added, "the mission of the church is the greatest enemy of
the Gospel."

So, clearly, all the slogans had failed—and also the restructuring
along multilateral lines—at least in the eyes of the younger churches.
Let us look, therefore, very briefly, at some of the issues at stake here.

The Roots of the Call

It seems to me that the usual way in which a younger church developed towards a new relationship with the corresponding sending church or agency was along the line of an increasing number of responsibilities being transferred to the younger church. The famous Venn-Anderson "three selves" formula also presupposed this kind of educational thinking.

The assumption seemed to be that the older church inevitably stood in a position of authority; the younger church would increasingly get a greater say in its own affairs until the stage was reached where it could go its own way. All this was just accepted policy, in spite of Roland Allen's pleas that something was wrong somewhere. The unquestioned assumption remained that ecclesiastical sovereignty, like its political counterpart, was something that could be subject to negotiation, or in the event of the older church being unwilling to give up control, something which could be obtained by way of a kind of UDI, a unilateral declaration of independence. It appears, therefore, that the end result of the process, in spite of everything said to the contrary, was not greater interdependence but increasing alienation.

The New Testament picture of interchurch relationships is the exact opposite, where Paul and others used their energy to make the churches all the more dependent upon each other. But, of course, the vital difference was that, in those days, mission was not a moving from the "haves" to the "have nots"—in fact, often it was the very opposite of that. But when, since the beginning of the Constantinian dispensation, the Church became a power base and the warden of culture and civilization, the problems we have today were bound to develop. However much we tried, the younger church remained, as Walbert Bühlmann puts it, "a Kindergarten for mother church and a poorhouse for the exercise of her charity" (1977:23). The Western church just remained captive to a donor mentality.

This is especially evident if we look at the increase in missionary personnel and finances. The more the younger churches became independent, so-called, the more missionaries were poured into the Third World. In Africa alone—where the moratorium call is most clearly sounded—the foreign missionary force has increased fourfold since 1910, from 11,000 to over 40,000. In the Republic of South Africa, which is in any case one of the most missionized territories in the world, there were, in 1973, no less than 5800 expatriate Roman Catholic Church workers and 1400 expatriate Protestants.

What goes for personnel goes for money too. In the three years between 1972 and 1975, financial support for mission in the USA and Canada increased by almost 60 percent from $393 million to $656 million. Thus the extent of Western church involvement in the Third World is experienced as suffocating and overwhelming. The younger churches feel that they are in reality moving in reverse, in spite of all the token language about new relationships. The overpowering resources of the Western world have a strangling effect on them.

To this must be added that the younger churches, being as human as we are, experience it as the way of least resistance to accept the generosity of the West. Consequently, some say that these churches need moratorium to protect them from themselves. To illustrate this the Black South African, John Thorne, recently used a striking image. He referred to the cunning way in which South African farmers used to catch baboons. A hole just large enough for the baboon's hand was cut in a large pumpkin. The animal would naively stick his hand in to grab the delicious seeds, but would not be able to withdraw the closed hand; the animal would sit there a prisoner until the farmer came and shot it. What it never realized was that it had to let go of the pumpkin seeds before it could withdraw its hand. The younger churches today, said Thorne, experienced the same problem. They were the prisoners of history and were not prepared to surrender the temporary comforts for the sake of their own survival (1977:34–35).

He then modified the metaphor of the baboon a little. In some national parks, he said, visitors are handed a brochure on which appears a picture of a begging monkey. Alongside is printed a request: "Don't be cruel to monkeys: be kind to them and don't feed them. If you do, you rob them of the power to fend for themselves."

So the problem is not just one of the West's "donor mentality," but just as much one of a "receiver mentality" in the younger churches. In an essay in *Missiology* (3:15), the African Ogbu Kalu referred to the "Peter Pan syndrome," Peter Pan being the boy who never grew up. In the same way there are churches who never grow up but remain dependent children. Only a radical moratorium would free them from this trap of dependency.

Sometimes the moratorium call is directed primarily at the missionaries themselves who are unable to foster meaningful relationships. Mission is a way of expressing our love to our fellowmen, but as Byron Haines has pointed out, "When we do seek to love, even here the object of our love is often the neighbor or enemy who does not seriously threaten our material security or challenge our particular way of viewing life and faith" (1973). In light of this the Black Methodists for Church Renewal have, some years back, issued an urgent challenge to the Mission Board of the United Methodist Church in the USA, in which they said:

> The Board of Missions must now bring home all of its 1400 missionaries for a domestic training course of at least five years, working with the alienated poor in the U. S. This would represent a serious effort to cease the imperialist domination of other cultures and would make possible the necessary process of indigenization and self-determination of all Third World citizens (n.d.:57–58).

And then there is exported Western denominationalism which, in effect, guarantees continued dependence on the West. Every denomination in almost every African country has its own seminary, printing press, and ecclesiastical headquarters, while various pastors from competing churches work in the same village, each with a small, hardly viable congregation. So these little churches can, in fact, only operate as long as they remain dependent on overseas help. But would they not, perhaps, if left alone, be forced to unite their efforts and rationalize them?

Of course, it would be easy to muster a formidable army of arguments against the idea of moratorium. Is it not, for instance, impractical and unattainable given the poverty of some Third World countries? Even more serious,: is it not irresponsible in light of the three billion non-Christians in the world today? Does it not, also, imply a very unfair judgment on the missionaries, simply following the "myth of the sinless victim," where all blame rests with the missionaries and none with the leaders of the younger churches? Is not, moreover, the call for a moratorium in reality a betrayal of the catholicity of the Church? Is the missionary not needed as a symbol of the universality of the Church, the representative of the ecumene on the local level? Lastly, could it perhaps be that the proponents of a moratorium are confusing the motivating forces of Christianity and nationalism and allowing the younger churches to develop into the theological arm of political movements?

All these are serious questions which demand careful and penetrating answers. I am not going to try to provide these here. But I would like to say that when all these answers have been given, logically and theologically correct, and when all has been said and done, the real issue might still have remained untouched. We might still not have penetrated the profundity of the moratorium call. At its deepest it is a cry that says, "Please hear us. Please take us seriously!"

This is the same cry as the one sounded by Azariah at the Edinburgh Conference when he concluded his panegyric on what the missionaries had done, using the words, "But we ask you to give us more than all this. Give us FRIENDS!" And, as Steven Neill once remarked, in the sober pages of the Edinburgh Report that last word is printed in capital letters. So Azariah must have said it very loudly and clearly!

Kefa Sempangi of East Africa recently said to a missionary conference in this country, "Send us brothers and sisters, not missionaries and missions!" The Bangkok conference has also put it well, "The whole debate in the moratorium springs from our failure to relate to one another in a way which does not dehumanize." This means that if we don't find a solution on that level, all other arguments about the feasibility and desirability (or not) of a moratorium really remain beside the point.

Elements of True Mutuality

The solution, I believe, can only be found when the churches in the West and those in the Third World have come to the realization that each of them has at least as much to receive from the other as it has to give. This is where the crux of the matter lies. The real problem is, as G. A. Hood puts it, "that some parts of the Church are clearly being impoverished by feeling unable to give and others by their inability to receive" (1972:277). We know that in ordinary human situations, genuine adult relationships can only develop where both sides give and receive.

We have known that all along, I suppose. That is why there has been so much talk—and surely not just talk but also action—about mature relationships, partnership in obedience, and the like. It seems to me, though, that the fatal mistake we usually made was that we saw this exchange, this process of giving and receiving, as having to take place in respect of the same kind of "commodities." The West has to receive from the younger churches what it gives to them. Now we know that the "commodities" the Western church has to give are to be found especially in these areas: personnel, finance, and skills. Within these areas we share such commodities as technology, administration, theology, etc. The older churches have an abundance of these commodities and share with others out of this abundance.

In this process, two things are happening. The first is that we in the Western churches, in the areas indicated, operate within the framework of a mentality of being independent, of being able to go it alone and disregard others. Our mission is, as Orlando Costas has pointed out, a "mission out of affluence" (1973). Deep down in our hearts we believe we have enough to spare, not only financially, but also spiritually. We think, and the others sense that we think, that we are, in the last analysis, independent of them.

The other thing that happens in this process is that we embark on desperate efforts to achieve reciprocity, but this reciprocity is expressed, over and over again, in respect to the very same commodities of which we have an abundance. A minister from Ghana goes to work for a few years in a congregation in Switzerland; an Indian theologian is invited as guest lecturer to an American seminary. And behold! We have reciprocity! For in both instances both parties give and receive the same commodity.

The question, however, is whether this is not plain self-deception. If a church in Ghana lends two or three pastors to a Swiss church, and in the meantime dozens of church workers stream from Switzerland to Ghana, along with hundreds of thousands of Swiss francs, can the Ghanaian church truly pride itself in the reciprocity of the relationship?

I do not wish to assert that this form of reciprocity is unimportant. On the contrary, it is of the greatest importance. I do, however, wish to claim that it would be self-deception to let reciprocity stand or fall by such activities. We would, if we did so, postpone "mature relationships" indefinitely. Walbert Bühlmann notes that "according to the most optimistic calculations, developing nations will still need substantial foreign aid at the end of the present century. This will be true also of those churches which are no longer 'mission' but are still in need of help, 'developing churches'" (1977:378).

Naturally we must do all in our power to close this gap. And yet it is important to remember that closing this gap does not, in itself, guarantee true reciprocity; in fact, such reciprocity is not dependent upon the closing (or not) of the gap, nor on the question of who has the most to contribute in the area of finance, personnel, or skills. Genuine reciprocity can only develop where the two respective partners do not receive the same as they have given. In other words, does reciprocity not presuppose complementary?

Fine, we might say, but what do the younger churches truly have to give us? The missionary from the West usually knows exactly what he has to give: the faith, the message of salvation, education, health services, technology, social progress. He does not know as clearly what he has gone to receive. And that is where the trouble starts. We have to teach him to open his eyes to what he has gone to receive, not just what he has gone to give. And once his eyes have been opened to this, he'll be amazed at the quantity and quality of what he has gone to receive.

Gifts from the Younger Churches

Let us try to identify some of these areas. Can you visualize for a moment right now the Western church without the younger churches? How impoverished we would be; how caught up in our different brands of scholasticism; how isolated from one another! Isn't it true that the whole ecumenical movement began on the so-called mission fields, and to this day still draws its greatest inspiration from the younger churches? Was it not they who helped to take away the scales from our eyes so that we began to discover one another as brothers and sisters?

The apostle Paul ostensibly did not receive much from his Gentile congregations. He was always the one who gave to them. But is this picture entirely correct? Wouldn't it be correct to argue that Paul received as much as he gave? Are not the differences between Paul and Peter to a large extent due to the fact that Paul had discovered something of the truly universal meaning of the Gospel from his Gentile converts in the very act of his expounding that Gospel to them? Was his attitude about the at-most relative value of the Torah simply due to his own theological insights revealed directly to him by God, or was it also the result of his interchange with Gentile Christians? Did he not grow as much as they did? And is the same not true of the Western missionary and, via him, also of the Western churches?

Or look at some other areas. The renewal of the pastorate and of catechetics in the Roman Catholic Church actually began in the younger churches from whence it worked through to the older. Can the Roman Catholic Church in the West still picture itself without that impulse to renewal? Or take the matter of baptism. Walbert Bühlmann says, "For ourselves, baptized unresisting in infancy and confirmed as school children, we need to share their experience of the meaning and the shock of biblical metanoia" (1977:386). Likewise, it cannot be denied that it was the Third World churches which rediscovered the office of the believer—not only theoretically, but also in practice. These churches are for the most part churches of the laity in remote little congregations, some of which see a priest or pastor at most once a month or even once a quarter; yet divine worship and other activities go on uninterrupted.

These are only some of the many areas we have to become aware of—some of the many gifts which the younger churches can impart to the older by way of genuine reciprocity and interdependence. They are "commodities" we often do not have any more, yet of which we are in desperate need. And if we measure these against our contributions from the West—material aid, personnel, and all kinds of skills—then the real question to be put to us would perhaps be: who here is really the beneficiary and who the benefactor? Equally important: along this road we manage to get away from many of the current definitions of "partnership" which yield little more than lip service and camouflage while the one-way traffic continues to move steadily behind the facade.

The point is that we need the younger churches just as badly as they need us. No church can demand total autonomy for itself. If it does, it becomes a mere service station for its own clientele and thus a pseudo-church. But the missionary frontier is everywhere. At the most it is the nature of that frontier that varies from place to place. Twenty percent of the total population of Kenya now attends church on any Sunday morning; for Britain the corresponding figure is no more than five percent. Under such circumstances, where is the real mission frontier? Every church today faces need and crisis; every church is either still in the diaspora situation or is returning to it. And in the words of I Corinthians 12:26,27, "If one part of the body suffers, all the other parts suffer with it; if one part is praised, all the other parts share its happiness. All of you are Christ's body, and each one is a part of it."

Daniel T. Niles has suggested a striking metaphor. Mission, he says, is one beggar telling other beggars where to find bread. The point is that we are both beggars, and equally dependent on the bread. We have to share it with one another. As a matter of fact, it is only as we share it that we become fully aware of its true taste and its nutritious value. So we are not only dependent on that bread but also on those who share it with us.

We have often been told that true love consists in giving ourselves to others. That is not entirely correct. In fact, that kind of self-giving may lead to others feeling inferior and worthless. True love is, much rather, accepting that you are dependent on the other, expecting something from him. The best I can give somebody is not myself, but enabling him to become a giver. Is that not what Paul says in Ephesians 4:16? "Christ is the Head, and on him the whole body depends. Bonded and knit together by every constituent joint, the whole frame grows *through the due activity of each part,* and builds itself in love."

In conclusion then, I want to challenge myself and you as teachers of missiology. We tend, almost as a matter of course, to teach missiology as the subject about what we in the West can give to the churches in the Third World. What about introducing another emphasis, another perspective: making our students aware of the wealth we are constantly receiving from these churches and of how poor we would have been had we not had them as partners? If we really succeed in infusing this awareness and this spirit into our students and constituencies, we will, I believe, have solved not only the moratorium problem but also the whole delicate matter of what partnership and mutuality mean. We will have convinced the younger churches that we cannot go ahead without them, that they should not turn their backs on us but share their riches with us.

Endnote

1. The author wants to put on record that a study in Dutch by E. Jansen Schoonhoven (1977) has helped him considerably toward seeing the issues under discussion more clearly.

References Cited

Black Methodists. n.d. *Missionary Service in Asia Today.* Hong Kong: Chinese Christian Literature Council.

Bühlmann, Walbert. 1977. *The Coming of the Third Church: An Analysis of the Present and Future of the Church.* Maryknoll, NY: Orbis.

Costas, Orlando. 1973. "Mission out of Affluence." *Missiology* 1:405–423.

Haines, Byron. 1973. Book Review. *Al Mushir* 15:302.

Hood, G. A. 1972. "In Whole and in Part." *IRM* 61:269–280.

Kalu, Ogbu. 1975. "The Peter Pan Syndrome." *Missiology* 3:15–29.

Nacpil, Emerito. n.d. "Whom Does The Missionary Serve and What Does He Do?" *Missionary Service in Asia Today.* Hong Kong: Chinese Christian Literature Council.

Schoonhoven, E. Jansen. 1977. *Wederkerige Assistentie van Kerken in Missionair Perspectief.* Leiden: Inter-University Institute for Missiological and Ecumenical Studies.

Thorne, John. 1977. "Liberation as a Church Programme for Mission." *Out of the Dust: The Moratorium Debate,* M. Nash, ed. Braamfontein: South Africa Council of Churches.

Van Randwijck, S. 1958. "Some Reflections of a Mission Board Secretary." *The Ghana Assembly of the International Missionary Council.* London: Edinburgh House Press.

CHAPTER 8

Structures and Strategies for Interdependence in World Mission

Charles R. Taber

The vision of truly equal, truly interdependent brotherhood of Christians in mission is not a new one. Neill, for instance, points out that Bishop A. R. Tucker of Uganda (1890–1908) "envisaged a Church in which African and foreigner would work together in true brotherhood, and on a basis of genuine equality" (1964:26). I do not think this dream was ever made explicit in the thinking of Rufus Anderson, Henry Venn, and John Nevius, though it is possible that it may have been implicit. But as Neill says on the page already cited, "For the most part missionaries of almost all the churches were blind to this kind of possibility."

In recent years, a number of churches and missions have tried to give concrete expression to this vision. Most of these are very new, so it is premature to make a final evaluation. But, though the designers retain their enthusiastic high hopes, I would anticipate problems as these schemes develop because I see in most of them signs that the factors which tended to perpetuate dependence and to inhibit interdependence are more intractable than had been thought. Later we will look briefly at some of these experiments. In the meantime, let us look at the background issues.

The Practical Dimensions of the Problem

I will consider the practical dimensions of the difficulties we encounter in trying to foster interdependence under three headings: history, our conception of the task, and cultural differences. These of course interpenetrate and reinforce each other, so that the solution will of necessity be more complex and all-embracing than we might guess at first look.

Historical Background

It is of course true that the history within which we are forced to work, willy-nilly, is not of our making. But we cannot escape its far-reaching implications as the ground of many attitudes, formalized and institutionalized relationships, and entrenched patterns of behavior which constitute obstacles to our efforts.

For over four centuries, Europeans systematically conquered and exploited the indigenous peoples, first of the New World, then of Africa and Asia. Starting from essentially similar levels of affluence, power, and technological development in the fifteenth century, Western and non-Western societies have since experienced vastly different histories: the West has become unimaginably wealthy and powerful, the non-West has stagnated or worse. The major factors in the present disparity of status were colonialism, slavery, mercantilism, and all of the other terrible expressions of the West's oppression of the Two-Thirds World. Once the initial advantage was gained via relatively small innovations in navigation and weaponry, it was exploited to the hilt to augment in every way possible the ways in which the West could enrich itself at the expense of its colonies.

As we have by now heard *ad nauseam*—though without necessarily realizing its full implications for us today—the missionary enterprise coincided not only in time, but also in point of origin, and even largely in attitudes, policy, and methods with the colonial enterprise. This was true even in the occasional cases where missionaries vocally and courageously protested the grosser abuses of colonialism. The indigenous cultures, native societies, and individual persons were summarily assumed to be inherently inferior to their Western counterparts. In *all* relationships between Westerner and non-Westerner, authority and initiative, as well as the relevant skills and financial resources, belonged by definition to the Westerner. This sprang from and reinforced in the Westerner a deep-seated arrogance, and in the non-Westerner led to a combination of excessive deference, dependency, self-denigration, and resentment. Since we are still today experiencing the difficulty of overcoming similar problems arising from analogous causes among various ethnic minorities in the U.S.A., we should be prepared to see why this heritage cannot be forgotten overnight.

The ostensible end of the colonial era (1945–1975, focusing about 1960) and the beginning of national independence led to hopes of "freedom at last;" but these hopes have been rudely shattered as the West continues to dominate the Two-Thirds World by the power of its technological development and its enormous affluence. Working hand in glove, Western governments and Western corporations have established de facto control over the economies of the poorer nations.

The mechanisms involved include the contrast between the highly unstable prices of the raw primary commodities produced by the poor nations and the escalating prices of the finished products sold by the rich nations; the granting of loans at high interest rates, which burdens the bare treasuries of the poor countries, and with strings which ensure their use for purposes favorable to the wealthy nations' interests; and even the outright overt or covert intervention to "destabilize" unfavorable governments (e.g., Chile) and to establish or prop up oppressive regimes that favor the interests of wealthy countries at the expense of their own citizens. The poor countries are faced essentially with Hobson's choice: either they accept Western so-called "aid" and the burdens and controls it entails, or they opt for a meager level of self-reliance. In either case they find themselves unable to provide the basic services their peoples desperately need. The joint voices of the poor nations in the United Nations give them a forum, but their power is effectively neutralized by the vetoes of the big powers in the Security Council. So far, the production of petroleum is the only area where producers have been able in some measure to turn the tables on the rich nations by operating unitedly.

I have emphasized this point at such length because we must face the fact that, whatever our own attitudes and practices, this is the context in which we operate. Christian leaders in other countries are bright enough and informed enough to diagnose the problem; they are also aware that, by and large, the American Christian public sees nothing wrong with the present system. We are therefore obliged to prove ourselves before we can really win the trust which is the only basis on which interdependence can work.

Our Conception of the Task

A second area which causes us difficulties is how we understand the task and how we go about organizing and pursuing our goals. Here, ironically, it is the very abundance of certain kinds of resources in our hands which blinds us to potentially more fruitful ways of approaching the job. These matters are so intertwined that I will treat them together. We need to consider at least four aspects of this complex.

First of all, in almost all instances, **we assume from the outset that *we* know what the task is and what the goals are.** These are already defined in our minds and in our corporate deliberations and projections well before nationals are involved at all. After all, the mission has been working in a given area for many years; it has—at least one hopes—well defined goals; and of course it has set in motion processes and founded institutions and structures designed to achieve these goals. Seldom does one really open up all of these basic questions *de novo* when the national church or its agencies become involved. It is expected that they will work enthusiastically towards the goals we have set and take over willingly all the machinery we have built to reach them. My observation is that under such circumstances nationals at best feel ill at ease with the foreign patterns and institutions, and at worst completely uninterested and uninvolved. It is precisely this in turn which leads missions to conclude that nationals have no vision or initiative! We are, it seems, in a vicious circle. Way back in 1947, J. Merle Davis said, "The Western Church has made the mistake of girding the Eastern David in Saul's armor and putting Saul's sword into his hands. Under these conditions the Church on the mission field has made a brave showing, but it is reasonable to expect that it will give a better account of itself by using its own familiar gear and weapons" (Davis 1947:108).

More recently, reflecting a Third-World perspective and 25 additional years of frustrating experience, Byang Kato wrote: "One mission complained about a national church that reluctantly accepted an elaborate medical program only to sell it to the government and use the money for the felt need. While one does not want to sit in judgment on such a case, it is apparent that local involvement was lacking at the beginning" (Kato 1972:199).

One could quite legitimately ask, Why *should* Third-World church leaders simply take over from us without question all the precedents we have established? Are we so nearly infallible, and they so ignorant, that completely unbroken continuity is the best way to save God's mission? I doubt it.

Second, **our affluence has led us to develop the ecclesiastical analog of capital-intensive methods of work.** In *our* economy, the most expensive thing is human time, and any procedure or equipment which saves human time is an improvement. We have thus developed methods and techniques which require the large amounts of money we have at our disposal, and we unthinkingly give others the impression that is *the* way to do Christian work. In most of the rest of the world, equipment is prohibitively expensive, and the cheapest and most abundant resource is human time and strength. But we bypass the resource in which nationals are rich and major on the ones which we have in abundance. In such a "partnership" it is inevitable that the partner with the most highly valued resource will dominate.

This dominance is further buttressed by our conviction, to which we hold at least as firmly as we do to our doctrinal positions, that "he who pays the piper calls the tune" (Kalu 1975a:16). In other words, we accept without question the capitalist premise that in any operation the dominant factor is and ought to be the capital input rather than labor input. Under the guise of "accountability" and encouraged by our stereotypes about the undependability of nationals in money matters, we insist on retaining control of projects which we fund—including the covert control arising from the possibility of funds being cut off, the power of the implicit veto. I know of no greater single obstacle to true partnership than this attitude which we find so hard to relinquish. It is invariably mentioned when Third-World Christians discuss partnership or church-mission relations (Nacpil 1971; Costas 1973:415; Kalu 1975b; Kato 1972:197; see also Strong 1972:286; Taber 1976).

At the root of the problem is our materialism. This can be seen among Western donors, who will far more readily give for a building or an airplane than for true human needs. It can be seen in our priorities in business meetings at all levels, from the local church to denominational conferences to the board meeting, where questions of money and property tend to dominate the agenda. And it is of course reflected in our ready judgment, conscious or unconscious, that people who are poor are less important than people who are rich, and that societies that do not major in the accumulation of material wealth are backward.

That non-Westerners see this unlovely trait in us clearly is evident from two anecdotes. Loewen somewhere tells of a discussion with a group of Indians who told him that in their tradition the most important thing was spirits; but the Indians were learning from the missionaries to make money, not the Holy Spirit, the center of their lives. Some years ago, a missionary from Nigeria told me of a prominent American minister, well known in fundamentalistic circles, who visited Nigeria and spoke to a group of Nigerian ministers. The burden of his message was that because he served God, God had prospered him with a large salary, two cars, a big luxurious house, and so on. After the meeting, some of the Africans took my friend aside and asked him, "Is that man a Christian?"

Third is **our unbounded reliance on expertise, defined in technological terms and measured in years of formal schooling.** Our bemusement with expertise is reflected in our tacit assumption that *we* know how it ought to be organized, that *we* know how to plan and project and schedule. This, I think, is the reason we so spontaneously go about defining goals and methods unilaterally and only invite nationals to join in at a later stage. And if perchance we are willing to relinquish some of this technologically based power, it is because one or more of the nationals have been educated in the Western pattern and therefore have the same kind of expertise as we do. But not all missiologists are sure that this is a good idea. "Heaven save us," pleads John V. Taylor, "from an international Christian technocracy" (1971:337).

A subsidiary aspect of this attitude is our mania for specialization and compartmentalization. We have buildings which are used only on Sunday and other buildings which are never used on Sunday. By reflex the word "education" evokes for us a school, complete with specially designed building, specialized furniture and equipment, and specialized personnel. The word "worship," on the other hand, evokes a distinctive building, specialized furniture and equipment, and specialized personnel. This approach, especially in regard to buildings and equipment, multiplies the cost of the total operation.

Fourth, **this bedazzlement with money and expertise has right from the start subverted true indigeneity in the church,** and it continues to do so. Huge areas of the work—education, health care, development programs, etc.—are without question and almost by definition beyond the effective control of local churches. They lack the funds to support them and the professionals to run them, and so by design or by default foreign funds support them and foreign experts control them. In at least one Mennonite field, Zaire, 80 percent of the church budget comes from overseas and is almost exclusively devoted to these parachurch ministries and to the top-level administration of the church (Mutombo-Mpanya 1977). This situation, says Mutombo-Mpanya, results in tensions and jealousies between two classes of Christian workers: those engaged on local church ministries, who are supported at a modest level by their churches, and those engaged in the glamorous and heavily subsidized service or administrative ministries, who are supported at a much higher level by foreign funds.

While Dennis Clark was not writing specifically about this issue, his observations are, I think, extremely pertinent:

> The national staff member of a foreign-controlled mission faces serious problems. Financed and directed by a society heavily dominated by Westerners and whose first loyalty is to foreign supporters, he owes extraterritorial loyalties to that society. Often the result of this situation is alienation from local people… It seems almost too late for Western societies to recruit the national because, with very few exceptions, the stigma of being labeled a "stooge" or "puppet" reduces usefulness…The Western concept of "hiring and firing" overlooks the deep feeling of Christians in the Third World and can

only attract "hirelings" who will flee when the wolf comes (Clark 1971:207–208).

It is because of these difficulties that Kalu does not hesitate to call missionary education "an instrument of bondage" because "it bred marionettes in Church and State" (1975a:19).

To summarize: our approach to conceptualizing and organizing the task subverts true partnership because we unilaterally assume the right to define goals and methods, and because we rely on capital-intensive and technology-intensive patterns which put a premium on *our* resources rather than on the resources of the local church.

Cultural Foundations

All of the problems I have already mentioned have cultural roots and cultural implications; however, I think it will be useful for us to isolate specifically four cultural factors which seem to me to be especially pertinent.

First is **our generally manipulative attitude toward our environment,** whether physical or social. We prize mastery, we reward the ambition to dominate, we regard the solution of problems by subjugating their causes as the best way to deal with them; "aggressive" is an adjective with highly favorable connotation. Perhaps the best metaphor for this attitude is the bulldozer. Three quotations underline this point: **Far from considering adjustments to environment a virtue, they (missionaries) believe the efficiency of their work depends on bending that environment** (Scott 1975:181). Missionaries introduced a Western form of church based on a cash economy, and since the form did not fit the Philippine economy, they tried to fit the economy to the form by amateur aid programs and employment in miniature industries (Scott 1975:183).

A significant example of the contrast in method emerged during the preliminary planning of the first All Africa Churches' Conference, held at Ibadan in 1958. British and American "experts" had agreed that this was to be Africa's conference run in Africa's way. But when it appeared that African leaders intended to have no agenda but to allow the findings to emerge from free, informal discussion, the experts felt constrained to take a hand, and once again Western methods prevailed (Taylor 1973:22n).

A special instance of this pragmatic, utilitarian, triumphalistic attitude is our view of time, which leads us to be extremely impatient. This no doubt springs from our culturally conditioned understanding of such passages as Ephesians 5:16 ("Redeeming the time...," KJV) which we interpret to mean that we should not "waste time" but plow ahead on a predetermined course, no matter what. It is not clear to me that this is a universally valid interpretation; rather, it smacks of finding in the Bible justification for our own haste.

Second, I think, is **our culturally induced bluntness of manner, our readiness to confront directly people with whom we disagree and push our ideas against theirs.** This cannot help giving us an undue advantage over people who are culturally more polite, whose culture requires them to be more reticent and more oblique, who are expected to "save face" and to avoid confrontations. When a national fails to tell us to our faces that he disagrees with us, we too easily jump to the conclusion that he agrees with us, and we rush ahead with our plans. We are not tuned in to the far more subtle clues that other cultures provide when people disagree.

Not unrelated is the expectation, which we share with most nationals, that **when cooperative programs and partnerships are initiated, it is the nationals who will adjust** in matters of language, life-style, and so forth; they must for the best results become culturally Westerners. It is a tribute to their resiliency and flexibility that so many can make the adjustment and operate successfully on our turf without losing their bearings on their own. But why should programs and activities planned for and carried out in a non-Western society be designed in a Western setting and a Western idiom? Why should *we* not be the ones to adjust our cultural style? Yet it hardly ever happens; we live in our cultural cocoon, and when we invite nationals to work with us, we invite them to a limited participation in our cocoon rather than venturing out of it to meet them on their ground. Scott has some scathing words about this as he describes the cultural insulation of missionaries: "Unless he (the missionary) gets out of that spacesuit, he will never be able to cry on a Filipino shoulder, lock arms with a Filipino brother on a steep path, or taste the salt of Filipino tears" (1975:172).

Finally, I suggest that **the very title of our discussion reflects a Western bias:** "*Structures and strategies* for interdependence." Would not an African or an Asian look first to *relationships* between persons as the locus of success or failure? True, the relationships have been systematically undermined or destroyed by the factors of power and culture described above, and an African like Kalu recognizes this explicitly. And he would even insist that attention must be given to establishing a sounder systemic basis for fraternal relationships. But the systemic is the means to the relationship, not the other way around. What we should be seeking is *first,* a basis on which to build concrete and genuine expressions of our international *koinonia*; and *second,* approaches to doing a job.

Some Attempts at Solutions

I mentioned above that a number of attempts have been made recently to solve the problem and establish true partnership. At this point I will examine a few of these briefly.

United Methodist Church. The United Methodist effort is described by Harris and Patterson (1975). Under the rubric "Building Community in Mission," they mention nine programs or activities which their Board of Global Ministries and their churches are involved in: international itinerating teams in U.S. churches, recognition that education for mission is mission, involvement of U.S. ethnic minorities in global mission, development of more flexible patterns of U.S. missionary service, exploration of patterns for mission in the U.S., affirmation of the increased interest of the laity in missionary service, support for people in mission in their own countries, encouragement of the internationalization of the missionary presence, and participation in support of people's networks. All of these things are highly commendable; but aside from their being often expressions of aspiration rather than of reality, they reflect, as far as I can see, a totally unilateral view of the initiatives to be taken. There seems to be a minimum of involvement by non-Western Christians in the planning of the effort and little wrestling with the deep level problems I have described.

The KKKMI. The KKKMI (Strong 1972) is a group of European agencies working in Indonesia. Strong actually lists a number of caveats and recommendations rather than describing an ongoing program. For instance, he differentiates between "partnerships where one partner is strong and one is weak; where one partner is silent; partnership with limited liability; and partnership where everything is held in common, such as a family with a joint banking account" (281). In discussing the slogan of KKKMI ("Today we are partners"), he asks, "whether it is a statement of fact or hope" (281). He points out that the very term "churches overseas" creates an unhelpful dichotomy (282). When a mission and a church are partners, he says, there will be tensions, since each has by definition a different focus of interest; it is necessary that each have a policy to guide its work and that both policies apply to the same arena. When the policies differ, which should prevail? The situation is exacerbated when a board insists on uniform policies in a number of fields where the churches may have different policies. Strong feels that the board secretary is in the crucial position to make or break the partnership. By means of a pointed question, he suggests that churches ought to be involved in the selection of missionaries. Finally, he emphasizes the difficulty involved when "we all want to receive unearmarked money but tend to want to pass it on earmarked" (286).

The Lutheran Church in America. Vikner (1974) describes the work of the LCA. He offers as a framework for the history of the LCA missions the usual three-stage model: missionary dominance, local autonomy, and interdependence. But he still clearly takes it for granted that the LCA will unilaterally determine its role and its priorities in the world.

Conservative Baptists. Jacques (1973) outlines in some detail the approach of the Conservative Baptists in India, and especially in the Philippines. What emerged out of a history of tensions was a structure of "equal partnership" in which the mission and the fellowship of churches, each autonomous, agreed to work together through a system of committees in which they had equal representation. (The "business committee," however, which is responsible for "the internal concerns of the mission, such as missionary housing, car, furlough, and administration" remains unilaterally the prerogative of the mission). The two partners contribute financially as each is able to a joint budget.

A lengthy document entitled "An Agreement for the Cooperative Stage of Nationalization of Conservative Baptist Work in the Philippines" spells out the name, the purpose, the goals, the members, the officers, the responsibilities, and so forth. Apparently the nationals were far more involved in the initial planning here than in the cases mentioned above. Though Jacques claims that the system works, it seems to me that there remains a good bit of insistence on the respective autonomy of the cooperating bodies, of keeping each other at arm's length, of leaning over backward to make sure each has exactly half of everything. To be sure, this is much better than fighting; but it is not true partnership in my understanding of the term. And the design of the whole scheme is extremely Western.

Joint Apostolic Action in Dahomey. Ayivi (1972) describes a cooperative effort called *L'Action Apostolique au Dahomey.* Proposed originally by Pastor Jean Kotto, general secretary of the Evangelical Church of Cameroun, it joins in a common project the Paris Missionary Society and a number of churches in francophone West Africa.

The focus of the project was to send a joint team representative of the churches involved and to incorporate a diversity of technical skills and specialization (theology, social work, education, nursing, agronomy, etc.) to one of the more resistant societies in West Africa, the Fon of Dahomey (now Republic of Benin). The threefold objectives were the development of the whole human being, the creation of a new form of Christian community, and the relating of African culture to the gospel. I do not have detailed or recent information on this effort; but though Ayivi in 1972 was cautiously optimistic, it is my impression that the effort has lost its elan. It is possible that the continued resistance of Fon society was a factor; I have also heard that the members of the team were not fully able to coordinate their efforts to work toward well-understood joint goals. At any rate, the project today is not living up to original hopes.

The Latin America Mission. The fullest and most satisfactory definition of partnership I have seen is that of Roberts (1973) concerning the Latin America Mission. In some respects they had already achieved some of the positions that others only hoped for, but they were still not satisfied. Roberts points out that preparation for this advance went back to 1950 when the late Kenneth Strachan began insisting on eliminating racial discrimination between Latins and North Americans at all levels of the LAM. But, says Roberts, this was not enough: "Latin American leaders tended to become frustrated. Instead of the rest of us becoming more Latin American in our attitudes and administrative style, the Latin missionaries were forced to conform to North American standards of candidate screening, missionary support, deputation activities, executive procedures and administrative style" (338).

Finally, a joint consultation was held in January 1971 at which the majority were Latins. Roberts recalls, "Perhaps most important of all...we learned...that the process of "latinamericanization"...did not consist simply in the recruitment of Latin Americans to serve side by side with us. We discovered that an organization might have 90 percent Latin Americans and still be a thoroughly "gringo" structure...The key, we found, is in the decision-making process. This process must be shifted to Latin America and controlled by Latin Americans if the organization is to become truly autochthonous" (339–340).

One aspect of the overall reorganization is a high measure of decentralization, and the granting of a high degree of autonomy to the various specialized ministries and institutions formerly operated by the LAM. The umbrella organization is the Community of Latin American Evangelical Ministries.

Roberts discusses frankly problems involved in determining budgets, public relations (especially with the US supporting constituency), personnel, and the transfer of properties. He mentions a tendency for divisiveness among the components of CLAME and difficulty in establishing solid internal communications.

The weakest part of the scheme, from my perspective, and one which makes the model less useful than it might otherwise be, is failure to mention the role of *churches* in the whole operation. This is a failure one might expect from the "faith mission" context; yet it is in my view a grave weakness in the pattern.

Summary

As I read these accounts, I am struck by the persistence of the underlying difficulties. They seem to have numerous incarnations and to surface in many manifestations. In summarizing this section of my paper, I can do no better than quote three people who have faced the issues involved very concretely. After a discussion of the old-fashioned direct control via the purse strings, Orlando Costas says, "While much of this may be changing, there are signs that point in the direction of more subtle, indirect controls. This may be seen even among the most advanced and progressive mission organizations. Even though they may have handed over all administrative and strategic control, their leaders always manage somehow to get their way" (1973:414).

Tom Hanks, a student worker in Latin America, vividly underlines the difficulty.

I had thought of paternalism as a deadly thing which I must be very careful not to create in my relations with students, instead of recognizing that it is the dominant, strangling pattern of relationships that exists in the church in Latin America. It is not that the student worker must be wise enough not to create such a monster. Rather he must be courageous enough to destroy the monster that now exists...Anyone who has read or seen the film Elsa, the lion who was "Born Free," knows it is infinitely easier to leave an animal free than to domesticate it and then try to teach it to be "indigenous."...You may even convince yourself that you have an indigenous student work—with students dashing all over putting your ideas into practice. Then dawns the day when you ask yourself, "But when was the last time they came up with a good original idea and carried it out?" and you realize it is not that they can't, it's that I'm dominating (1972:153–154, 156,157).

Finally, Emerito Nacpil explains why despair at this point led him to call for a moratorium on missionaries and foreign funds:

Of course, we can argue that we are not limited to these alternatives (with respect to whether the missionary serves mission or church, etc.). Instead, we can become partners—partners in obedience, joint participants in a common enterprise. But can we really? If we can, under present conditions, it can only be (and so far this seems to be the case) a partnership between the weak and the strong. And that means the continued dependence of the weak upon the strong, and the continued dominance of the strong over the weak, notwithstanding our efforts and protestations to the contrary. Under this kind of partnership, the missionary becomes the apostle of affluence, not sacrifice; cultural superiority, not Christian humility; technological efficiency, not human identification; white supremacy, not human liberation and community (1971:359).

I suppose one could sum up the whole matter in terms of the well-known recipe for elephant-rabbit stew: You take one elephant and one rabbit. We should not be surprised when the "50-50" stew in fact tastes more of elephant than of rabbit!

Dimensions of a Solution

I am not in a position to offer you a well-integrated model of the ideal form of interdependence. I can, however, suggest some features which I think will characterize any successful model.

Mutual Trust. Fundamental to any success is a climate of mutual trust, respect, and genuine Christian love (i.e., love shorn of its paternalistic, condescending dimension), based on an understanding of the *koinonia* God intends for the whole body. Since this is basic, and since we easily confuse biblical ideals with concrete achievement, I want to quote Ogbu Kalu briefly. "It seems quite clear that no amount of tinkering with the present pattern will work. A missionary may be fully aware of the theological nature of the Church as the Body of Christ and the biblical pattern of interrelationships as one of mutual responsibility and interdependence. Yet he cannot avoid being paternalistic. The source of paternalism in mission is the structure of the enterprise itself" (1975b:143–144).

In other words, it is far from enough to realize fully the theological-biblical dimensions of a solution; we have to work in the concrete situation to find concrete expressions for the spiritual reality, which implies, for Kalu, the demolition of a system which inherently works at cross-purposes with the biblical pattern. It is this fact, according to Kalu, which underlies calls for moratorium, not in rejection of the Great Commission, but in explicit obedience to it. Only when the young churches are given breathing room, when the inherently oppressive presence of the mission is removed or relaxed, can they find their true role in the ministry of the total body.

Local Decision Making. It is crucial that decision making be focused in the place and on the persons who will be most directly involved. In other words, partnership involves each partner group having *primary* responsibility and authority in their own sphere, and *then* helping others in their spheres (Arias 1971:252). In other words, just as we do not expect African Christians to take unilateral or even primary initiatives with regard to churches in the U.S., so we should not arrogate to ourselves the right to initiate decisions and programs in other parts of the world. Kalu underlines this when he says, "The nature of the Universal Church means that aid relationships among churches must be different from aid relationships among nations. If there is to be real sharing-in-common, there must be sharing-in-common of power" (1975a:22).

As long as Westerners remain effectively in charge of designing the program, there will continue to be difficulties with the *model* of development used, and with the *mode* and *priority* of aid.

At this point I would like to comment on the suggestions of Calvin Shenk (1977) and Gerald Keener (1977). Shenk suggests the substitution of multilateral relations for bilateral ones. There is much value in this, but it is not by itself a full solution. The United Bible Societies entered into a radically centralized system called the World Service Budget for the express purpose of obviating the patron-client relationship between the big societies and local offices and specific projects overseas. But it turned out that the dominance of the big societies remained securely in place. Bible Society operations that received funds from the World Service Budget, even in countries with "autonomous" Bible Societies that were full members of the UBS, were subject to line-by-line review or veto by UBS executives, while the societies which were financially self-supporting did as they pleased. Efforts were made to modify this invidious distinction by making the financial operations of the big societies open for inspection, but there was never any question of bringing them under the tutelage of the UBS. The same distinction exists today in the appointment of senior personnel: ABS or BFBS can appoint whom they please to any internal post, but the Bible Society of Ghana cannot appoint a general secretary without the approval of the UBS.

Keener's proposal that *churches* enter into a direct partnership across the seas is also good, but by itself a bit idealistic. Churches separated not only by thousands of miles but by enormous cultural gulfs need knowledgeable brokers to establish and maintain sound communications. Granting the fact that the churches are the fundamental reality, mission agencies can usefully serve this linking function if they are properly set up to do it.

Encouraging Local Initiative. Following from the above, we need to encourage nationals to take the lead in determining the most fundamental goals and methods of operation. We need to ask them, and press them for an answer. "What do *you* think are the tasks of the church?" And when they have sorted out *their* understanding of their mandate from God, we will need to encourage them to design methods which are appropriate to their setting and their resources. This will need to be done with all aspects of the work. If, for instance, they decide that the church needs to have educational activities, they need to be free to question whether this implies a school in our sense at all. In this game, we need to realize that by definition *they*, not we, are the experts; our expertise relates to a very different world, and is, as we have seen above, often a hindrance rather than a help when exported.

I realize that we cannot actually start with a blank slate on which to write beautiful new programs; we cannot at once eliminate all the mistakes of the past. At this point I can only repeat my advise in *The Other Side:* A truly Christian approach in the field will begin with the mission taking the initiative. Mission boards need to approach their national churches with the following kinds of statements:

1. We acknowledge and confess that our financial operations are sub-Christian. Please forgive us.

2. Let us together examine the whole program that we have instituted, most of which was instituted without consulting you. Let us prayerfully see which parts of the program have been genuinely helpful to you and which parts exist only because some missionary might be offended if they were discontinued. Let us see which parts of the program you would have instituted on your own initiative if we had not been in control.

3. Let us with all deliberate speed eliminate those programs which do not contribute sufficiently to the well-being of the church to justify their cost in money and freedom of action.

4. Let us plan how the remaining programs can reflect the Holy Spirit's leading in this specific sociocultural and historical situation. You take the initiative since this is your church under God. We are God's servants for your sake.

5. Finally, let's discuss finances honestly, see what is needed and discover together where it will come from—how much from local sources, how much from outside. We pledge to you that we will truly relinquish control (Taber 1976:43–44).

Giving Without Strings. The last sentence spells out the next feature of a successful partnership: that giving be truly without strings. This was implicit in the quotation from Kalu on church aid; it is underlined by this deeply felt statement of Byang Kato: "If foreign aid is to help rather than hinder the work of the Lord, it must be given as unto the Lord and received as God's money. There must be a strong element of trust all around... Missionaries...should have confidence in the nationals. The commonly heard phrase, 'You cannot trust the national,' must be dropped and humble repentance offered for the past action" (1972:197).

The only way this can be put into effect, I think, is for us to repent of and grow out of our materialism, that materialism which leads us to grossly overestimate the importance of the financial component of the operation (what we contribute) and to underestimate the value of the human component (what nationals contribute), the materialism that in the name of "accountability" will not relinquish control of programs to which we have given money, the materialism that prevents us from trusting nationals.

Can We Become Poor?

Perhaps an even greater revolution of values is called for. Weiser, in a tantalizing allusion (1975:134), suggests that Jesus in Luke 9:3 ("Take nothing with you for the trip...") had in mind a purpose relevant to our discussion: "With all the necessary allowances made for the different socioeconomic context of the Gospels this injunction to the disciples seems to be designed to put them into a state of extraordinary powerlessness in any economic context." This raises the question for us: is it possible for us to really become functionally poor and weak in our dealings with Third World churches? What would we have to renounce in a very concrete way to free these churches from our overwhelming combination of powers which oppress them: the history of colonial relations, our financial affluence, our technological expertise, and our assumption—which they are in no position to deny effectively—that these powers give us the right to determine their destiny?

Epilogue

After the discussion of my paper in Hillsboro, I feel constrained to make explicit two points which were implicit in my thinking but which obviously did not come through to everyone.

First, the reason I shied away from becoming more specific in proposing solutions is precisely because, beyond the generalities I outlined, each situation is to a great extent unique, and solutions must be sought in *concrete* contexts and in interaction with *specific* persons and groups. There would have been a remainder of subtle imperialism in our sitting as a group of North Americans in Hillsboro and offering universal solutions to be applied. A crucial part of the solution is the dialogue process by which the solution is discovered and applied, and one cannot predict from a distance what will emerge. One must play it by ear (to speak in purely human terms), or be sensitive to the contextual guidance of the Holy Spirit (to use biblical categories); and the guidance must come to the persons and groups involved in *joint* prayer, confession, and discussion.

Second, in spite of my harping on problems and difficulties, I am essentially optimistic about *possibilities*; but my optimism is not based on our insight or our technical competence, but only on God's grace. I cannot be triumphalistic about solving problems through scholarship and expertise, because if I am, these will become yet more tools of manipulation. But I can and do have confidence in God to transcend our limitations and sins.

The condition on our part is repentance for our sins. We have a tendency to want to pass through this stage quickly and to see in advance a blueprint for a happy outcome beyond the repentance to make it worthwhile; otherwise, we feel, the repentance will have been in vain! However, biblical repentance cannot be instrumental in that sense; it dare not be minimized or bypassed, and there is no guarantee of "success" on the other side. But we also need to see that *metanoia* is not self-flagellation or wallowing in guilt (which would lead to self-pity and eventually to self-congratulation!); rather, it is an honest facing up to our guilt, a repudiation of the sinful patterns (which will have systemic and structural consequences, as Kalu pointed out), and a determination to look ahead to the *possible* future God has in store for us (first person plural inclusive, i.e., Western and non-Western Christians). In other words, *metanoia* is a liberation from the shackles of past sins and *for* a better future. But we need to realize that our non-Western partners, not being able to see our hearts as well as God does, may take more convincing than God does that we mean what we say. So they may put us to the test in a variety of ways. But I firmly believe in the vision of "one new humanity" that John Toews so ably outlined for us.

References Cited

Arias, Mortimer. 1971. "Mutual Responsibility." *International Review of Missions* 60:249–258.

Ayivi, Emmanuel. 1972. "Joint Apostolic Action in Dahomey." *IRM* 61:144–149.

Clark, Dennis E. 1971. "Receiving Churches and Missions." *Evangelical Missions Quarterly* 7:201–210.

Costas, Orlando E. 1973. "Missions Out of Affluence." *Missiology* 1:405–423.

Davis, J. Merle. 1947. *New Buildings on Old Foundations.* New York/London: SCM Press.

Hanks, Tom. 1972. "Paternalistic—Me?" *EMQ* 8:153–159.

Harris, Ruth M., and Patterson, Patricia J. 1975. "People in Mission: Toward Selfhood and Solidarity." *IRM* 64:137–142.

Jacques, Edwin E. 1973. "An Equal Partnership Structure." *EMQ* 9:65–73.

Kalu, Ogbu U. 1975a. "The Peter Pan Syndrome." *Missiology* 3:15–29.

————. 1975b. "Not Just New Relationship but a Renewed Body." *IRM* 64:143–147.

Kato, Byang. 1972. "Aid to the National Church—When it Helps, When it Hinders." *EMQ* 8:193–201.

Keener, Gerald H. 1977. "Critique of 'Internationalization of Mission.'" *The Seminarian* 7(5):3.

Mutombo-Mpanya, 1977. "Problems of the Churches in Central Africa." Paper delivered at symposium on "The Church in Africa." Milligan College, 31 March, 1977.

Nacpil, Emerito P. 1971. "Mission but not Missionaries." *IRM* 60:356–362.

Neill, Stephen C. 1964. *A History of Christian Missions.* Middlesex/Baltimore: Penguin.

Roberts, W. Dayton. 1973. "Mission to Community—Instant Decapitation." *IRM* 62:338–345.

Shenk, Calvin E. 1977. "Internationalization of Mission." *The Seminarian* 7(5):1–3.

Strong, Robbins. 1972. "Practical Partnership with Churches Overseas." *IRM* 61:281–287.

Taber. Charles R. 1976. "Money, Power and Mission." *The Other Side,* March-April 1976, 28–34, 43–44.

Taylor, John V. 1963. *The Primal Vision.* London: SCM Press.

———. 1971. "Small is Beautiful." *IRM* 60:328–338.

Vikner, David L. 1974. "The Era of Interdependence." *Missiology* 2:475–488.

CHAPTER 9

Hindrances to Cooperation:
The Suspicion about Finances

Lausanne Committee for World Evangelization

Money makes headlines. Religious convictions, organizational rivalries, or personal jealousies rarely hit the news like those matters which concern the financing of Christian ministries. Perhaps no other topic comes anywhere near this one in eliciting comments of derision from a watching world. Such adverse reports serve only to confirm their prejudices and reaffirm their "wisdom" of keeping away from organized religion. Reports of this nature also increase public suspicions of innocent religious groups, whose image becomes tarnished through the world's lumping together of "religious hypocrites."

Scandals are increasing by the year. Competition for the mighty dollar gets keener by the month. Because the questionable techniques of the minority bring scorn on the rest, the Commission recognizes that this type of problem does more to hinder cooperation in evangelism than most, if not all, of the problems already discussed.

We feel this general deterioration should be seen in its setting and wish to present some facts for the consideration of Christian leaders, prior to discussing more specifically three clear categories of problems in this area.

The Current Situation in Christian Giving

There appears to be a chain of trends and events which has created a stronger spirit of competition for the Christian dollar in both church and parachurch organizations:

(i)   For centuries, Christians considered the local church as the only "storehouse" for their tithes and offerings (Mal. 3:10).

(ii)   Independent missions and interdenominational organizations have more recently staked their claim to a share of the pie.

(iii)   As materialism increases, luxury and selfishness usually reduce the individual's desire for sacrificial giving.

(iv)   The dramatic increase in the number of parachurch ministries means that available funds must be divided into yet smaller portions.

(v)   The recent epidemic of inflation and economic recession, resulting in a lower discretionary income, has further reduced some people's ability to give. This is often caused by a strong desire to maintain living standards.

(vi)   Increasingly ambitious corporate goals, in church and parachurch alike, make the spirit of competition more determined than ever.

Consequences of This Chain of Events

(i)   Questionable fund-raising techniques and subtle exploitation begin to infiltrate so-called Christian organizations.

(ii)   Interorganizational squabbling and public disgust bring shame and disgrace on the work of the gospel.

(iii)   Attempts to resolve these major hindrances to cooperation in evangelism seem powerless, in the face of determined human selfishness.

(iv)   Empire after empire has experienced a similar cycle of events prior to irreversible decadence and collapse.

(v)   Only God the Holy Spirit can produce the humility, meekness, patience, forbearance, and love which will slow down the pace of deterioration and the rate of decay.

These statements are not intended to be the cry of a prophet of doom, but rather an attempt to face realistically the context in which we must tackle the problems which hinder cooperation in evangelism. This backdrop will, hopefully, give greater incentive for responsible action, as we seek to resolve the tensions relating to financial concerns.

In otherwise equally caring societies, citizens of lesser developed countries are more willing to sacrifice than their counterparts in wealthier countries. Wealth and materialism, rather than extending a helping hand, more frequently exhibit a clenched fist of determination to hold on to treasured possessions. History has witnessed this phenomenon time and again. It inevitably leads to those brief decades of decadence which immediately precede the departing of a nation's glory. Governments decrease the percentage of the Gross National Product available for helping poorer nations, and individuals become increasingly inward-looking and self-serving.

World hunger telethons throughout North America in recent years provide ample evidence that up to ninety percent of those responding to the needs of a suffering humanity live in the poorer socioeconomic areas of a city or region. Minority ethnic communities are particularly responsive, while refugees, uprooted from their homelands and deprived of their possessions, are often the most sympathetic of all.

The last decade has seen the institutionalized church in the Western world seriously questioning the mushrooming of organizations as well as the fund-raising techniques employed. Some of the more serious allegations involve the apparent lack of ethical principles behind ceaseless cries for help from those who will otherwise go under in their struggle to survive. Particularly singled out by an increasingly unsympathetic public are alleged instances of wrongful exploitation they feel take place in certain mass media ministries. Those with a genuine involvement in these fields are then suspect because of the publicity given to the offenders.

Problems Which Can be Resolved by Pastors and Boards of Local Churches

Pastors and church boards have frequently shown insensitivity to the validity, usefulness, and financial needs of parachurch ministries. Sometimes through an inadequate ecclesiology, but often from a narrow parochial vision, certain local churches (like horses harnessed and blinkered) seem unable to see beyond the confines of their own work. Consequently not only is parachurch support at the bottom of the missions priority list, but church members are positively discouraged from giving to anything outside.

The wealthier a nation becomes, the more the spirit of worldly thinking can grip its churches. As a result, the success of a pastor or a local church is frequently judged in quantitative—and especially—economic terms. Pressure is put on him to achieve, and prove himself by increasing the church's budget. Sometimes this takes priority even over the feeding of the flock. His job is at stake. His peers are competing. His denominational head office is pressing. He will ultimately be judged a success or a failure on his ability in this activity, whether he is a godly man or not. Consequently, the first signs of anyone competing for these funds spell danger. He urges his people to be loyal and uses every opportunity to remind them of their responsibility to bring *all* the tithes into the storehouse (by which he means the local church). This also affects his attitude and actions towards other Christian ministries. Having noted the interest shown by the congregation in the organization whose director preached last Sunday evening's sermon, he fears lest such magnanimity on his part will open the door to a leak in the giving patterns of the congregation. He sometimes decides never again to open his pulpit to "the competition."

In spite of these efforts, he finds he has little control over the appeals for funds that pour day after day into the mailboxes of his congregation. While some members are influenced by his urgings, others are deeply moved by the newsletters from organizations. He appeals to them at least to channel their gifts through the church so that they are included in its missions disbursements. Later, however, a brief glance at the monies literally going through his fingers lets him know just how much the church is losing. He sometimes adopts new methods to stem the flow. He has even been known to pass on information which tends to put the recipient ministries in a bad light. Extremes in doctrine, personality conflicts, or excessive travel are but a few of the tidbits he hopes will stop the leaks and help fill the church coffers once more.

Such a scenario is not as rare as some would have us believe; but the blame for it cannot all be laid at the pastor's door. The pressure of a growing number of organizations, the excesses of some agencies, and the demands of his church board have heavily contributed to the problem, and he has succumbed. He has allowed his gaze to be distracted from the glory of God, the person of Christ, and the oneness of the Body. He has become competitive and partisan. Though that church may appear to flourish financially, it cannot but be impoverished spiritually. Expediency has replaced biblical principles, and selfishness taken over from liberality. Malachi 3:8 asks, "Will a man rob God?" As a commission, we wonder whether it could be that a pastor or elder who so vehemently opposes all extra-church organizational support does not rob God as much as the church member who spends God's portion on himself?

Problems Which Can be Resolved by the Leaders of Parachurch Organizations

It would be naive to think that the resolution of those matters pertaining to financial practices would alone result in churches more eagerly supporting parachurch bodies. Even those organizations with a spotless record in this area find they are by no means automatically put on to church budgets. Matters such as theology, validity, accountability, and personality, already discussed, contribute significantly to the malaise.

Nevertheless it would be true to say that the local church attitude toward parachurch groups would be far more healthy with the resolving of concerns to do with finance, resources, fund-raising, publicity, and overhead. The Commission grappled at length with some of these. And it is now our purpose to briefly discuss them, offering suggestions which could lead to better relationships in the work of world evangelism.

Obscure Financial Reporting. Although we have already considered the allegation that some voluntary agencies have inadequate accountability structures, the specifically financial aspects of such accountability frequently present a major problem to churches. While many organizations do have good accounting procedures, audited financial statements are not always made available to potential or existing donors. The Christian public, when they do receive them, often find them difficult to understand. This may be because organizations do not use a common format or because these statements often tend to allocate administrative or fund-raising expenses to "program" or "ministry," presenting a more healthy picture. The rationalizations for these questionable procedures are almost as numerous as the organizations involved. And those responsible often fail to see why the churches question the figures.

Alarming Overhead. Property upkeep and staff salaries often consume 50 percent or more of the income of a church. Yet a Christian organization is strongly criticized when its total administrative overhead exceeds even half of that. It seems that while a church has freedom to police the organizations (even publicizing its findings), the reverse is not considered ethical. While parachurch leaders are frequently asked about "responsible stewardship," many church buildings lie deserted for 165 out of 168 hours of each week. Furthermore, requests by various ministry groups for rented space in these buildings is more often turned down than approved. At a time when the Christian public is becoming increasingly aware of the administrative overhead of parachurch ministries, church boards could do much to further the cause of world evangelization by making facilities available at cost to groups doing the kind of work the church approves.

The Body of Christ is made up of people who vary greatly in the standards they demand of themselves and others. That diversity is evident, for instance, in their judgments regarding an organization's promotional and informational literature. Some are utilitarian at heart and fail to understand why anyone would use two colors on a printed sheet when one is cheaper. Others are highly selective in what they read, choosing mainly items that have appeal; they have little respect for things done shabbily or amateurishly. Parachurch personnel (as well as recipients of their publications) are representative of both categories. Each appeals only to a limited proportion of their constituents. We would urge Christian leaders to be sensitive to the standards and feelings of all God's people. Yet, while we would strongly discourage standards so low as to bring discredit on the gospel, we nevertheless deplore wasteful extravagances which contradict the very message we preach.

While the Commission understands the need for stressing the interrelationship of money, time, and energy, it regrettably notices that the life-style of some parachurch leaders leaves a lot to be desired if they wish to impress the Christian public with responsible stewardship. We need to be extra careful in differentiating between essentials and luxuries, perhaps especially in the area of travel. Christian people, including those who sit on church boards, are not blind to these things and can hardly be blamed when they express negative attitudes to those contemplating a donation to the organization concerned.

Unwise Use of Mailing Lists. The Commission is largely sympathetic toward those who find themselves placed on mailing lists without request or permission. While we recognize the difficulty in controlling this practice, we would do well to recognize that the public outcry against it has reached alarming proportions. The indiscriminate purchase or rental of mailing lists for ongoing use is not only unbecoming of those claiming Christian love which "has good manners" (Phillips), but also sinfully wasteful when it comes to the use of the Lord's money. With such practices in vogue among us, we need no longer wonder why mail frequently remains unopened or is discarded without being read. (This subject requires a more lengthy treatment by those who are specialists in the field.)

Another cause for public frustration is the low degree of importance given to requests to be removed from mailing lists. Those who grew up when standards of courtesy and morality were high often carry a continuing sense of guilt when they receive repeated requests for support they simply cannot give. They sometimes go to a lot of trouble to request deletion from a list, only to be ignored or kept waiting. Pastors are often their only resort, and the general impression is left that a leader who cannot be a wise steward of postage stamps is not to be trusted with larger amounts for ministry. Church leaders (who cannot normally use this method of appeal) find it easier to discourage giving than to graciously admonish the leader concerned.

Questionable Fund-Raising Techniques. Several items were of concern to the Commission:

(a) Distorted publicity

Whereas the integrity of most organizational leaders with regard to public information is questioned, the competition for the Christian dollar is so keen that distortions and exaggerations appear to be on the increase. Pictures can be deceiving and words are so flexible that wrong impressions can easily be conveyed even though every word of a newsletter may be justified.

Copy writers are sometimes guilty of playing the numbers game—as well as presenting an exaggerated picture of poverty, sickness, and disease. Surely the evidence of suffering and need is abundant enough without making it out to be worse than it really is.

We believe that scrupulous self-monitoring is essential, not only to prevent crippling legislation by governments, but primarily because the name of Christ and the cause of the gospel are both being compromised.

(b) Exploiting human need

The Commission expressed its conviction that some parachurch agencies should honestly examine their motivation in attempting to relieve the material needs of suffering peoples. While we unanimously laud all worthy efforts to bring compassionate aid to those in need, we equally deplore the questionable goals of those who often appear opportunistic and self-serving.

The world has never been more aware of all the warts on our globe. Modern technology enables us to receive crisis news within minutes and to dispatch relief-laden aircraft within hours. Whereas most human beings are born with a mechanism which sympathetically responds to human need, age produces a callusing of our emotions. We can watch the world's agonizing suffering on our television screens and sleep like babies after we switch them off. We have become accustomed to suffering. It now takes a crisis of alarming proportions to make us respond. When such a crisis occurs there seem to be two types of agencies that respond. The one, organizations who have been primarily called into being for these very humanitarian purposes and who go on working, unseen and unheralded, even when the television viewers have long forgotten; the other, organizations which came into existence for different—perhaps originally evangelistic—purposes, but who jump at the opportunity to climb on the popular bandwagon. None of us should be guilty of judging the motives of others. Yet all of us should avoid that kind of tugging at heartstrings which brings in support not only for the crisis, but to subsidize other unsupported programs. Some organizations are quite ill-equipped to bring relief and have been known to so frustrate the authorities that *bona fide* groups have suffered from the restrictions consequently imposed.

We, therefore, plead with leaders of agencies whose work is not primarily humanitarian to consider the consequences of their actions before they move. If there is any truth in the missionary slogan "God's work done in God's way will not lack God's supply," then let us redouble our efforts to do with excellence and vigor the work to which we have been called and for which we have been equipped. In this way, we shall win the respect of our supporting constituency.

(c) The spectacular and the dramatic

Akin to the foregoing is the peculiar bent of human nature to respond to that which is dramatic, secret, or otherwise exciting. Whereas the need to minister to those in countries "closed to the gospel" is very great, parachurch groups in particular can exploit the dramatic elements to such a degree that purses, wallets, and checkbooks spring to respond. Some of us wonder whether, because the popularity of some spectacular ministries is so high, it would be hard for the leaders to really pray that God would at last open the doors to a "closed" country; for if he did, the dramatic would be replaced by the routine, and giving would drop.

Yet again, although such groups are in the minority, they bring disrepute on the majority who are called by God to a difficult, dangerous and needy work. Once more we would plead with those so engaged to do nothing which is not completely open to the scrutiny of supporting Christians. We need to ceaselessly pray that whatever will most quickly extend God's kingdom will come about, whatever the effects on our current ministry. Nothing is more likely to win the respect and support of the churches, and thus further the cause of world evangelization.

(d) Inculcating unscriptural expectations

The Commission expressed concern over the policy (in a large number of parachurch groups) of offering some type of material reward to those who send a donation. We feel the motive for giving to God must be "because of the mercies of God" (Rom. 12:1) and not because of the book or record we will get out of it. We would discourage the "bubble gum mentality" of some donors who put the penny in the slot and wait for the goodies to come out. Our giving to God is not a "please" offering but a "thank" offering, and those who solicit funds should be careful, when offering something to the public, that they do not inculcate unscriptural expectations. Our failure to be corrected in this habit could result in our producing a generation of Christian children who will never give anything to God unless they get something out of it. Pastors who faithfully expound Scripture would be more supportive if organizations would teach by example the principles enunciated from the pulpit.

(e) Unrealistic goals

While long-term planning has now become an accepted part of institutional life, parachurch agencies sometimes ask for church criticism by setting unrealistic goals. A dream, a vision, or merely an over-optimistic nature can easily result in commitments which are unlikely to be met. When an over-ambitious leader finds that income is not enough to reach these goals, he may announce a crisis which puts unfair demands upon the Christian public. Sometimes pledges made to their churches have to be broken, in order for donors to refloat a sinking ship. Even then, it is not afloat very long before more trouble arises.

It is not surprising that pastors begin to wonder about the judgment (rather than the faith) of the parachurch leader. There is little doubt that people are attracted to men and women of vision. They enjoy reading of those who will take risks or work hard to accomplish great things for God. The mere announcing of unheard-of-goals will usually elicit a generous response from a large segment of the Christian Church. Some of our leaders are men and women of prayer, of faith and of sound judgment, who reach these goals and inspire confidence in the public. But the Commission expressed deep concern about those who, knowing the generosity of Christians towards exciting projects, announce that they are starting "to build a tower" (in "faith"), but who do not sit down first and properly "count the cost, whether they have sufficient to finish it" (Luke 14:28). In many cases, after they have "laid the foundation and are not able to finish it," they issue a crisis appeal to escape the judgment in the scriptural example that "all that behold it, begin to mock" them with the words, "this man began to build, and was not able to finish."

Whereas it has already been stated that a church strangle-hold on a parachurch agency can easily result in the destroying of initiative, it nevertheless appears to us that forging ahead in this manner without prior consultation is nothing short of irresponsible action, particularly when those not consulted are then called upon to bail out the project. Because of action based less on faith than presumption, the leader responsible now finds that he is not merely motivating but manipulating. This type of activity can hardly be expected to inspire confidence and build bridges of cooperation in the task of world evangelization.

Russ Reid, in an article entitled, "What Ruins Christian Leaders?— A plan for leashing top dogs," quotes U.S. Senator Mark Hatfield as saying:

> When I leave my office to go to the Senate floor, an elevator comes immediately...reversing direction if necessary and by-passing the floors of the other bewildered passengers aboard, in order to get me to the basement. As I walk down the

corridor, a policeman notices me coming and rings for a subway car to wait for my arrival and take me to the Capitol building—another elevator marked 'for Senators only' takes me to the Senate floor.

Reid continues:

These are words about power, about the rights and privileges bestowed on one who has placed himself into the rarefied air of Washington politics—where raw power is enshrined and seniority amply rewarded. Senator Hatfield has come to terms with his power, but he himself admits that the struggle not to abuse it never ends...

We don't need to be doing the nation's business to know what power is all about. Pastors of both large and small congregations have power. Deacons, elders, Sunday school teachers, and evangelists all have power...

Some of the most visible holders of power today are within the large, independent, religious organizations. Through their television ministries and direct mail systems, they wield tremendous influence. Unfortunately, this arena is also filled with the stories of Christian leaders who have built tremendous ministries, but who don't know how to exercise the power their Creator has given them. Their early vision—with its absolute dependence on God—often has shifted into a nightmarish one-man show. Unilateral seat-of-the-pants decisions upstage good counsel. 'The Lord told me to do it,' often becomes a pious platitude to justify leapfrogging over the wisdom of boards and committees.

Reid concludes:

These leaders aren't dishonest. They sincerely believe they're doing God's will. But what drives such leaders into mounting enormous debts for buildings, programs, and campaigns for which the need is very questionable?

(f) Unfair Solicitation

It is common knowledge that after having been placed on the missions budget of a supporting church, some Christian organizations then approach individual members of that church for further support. The Commission wonders whether this is not unfair, particularly if the pastor or budget committee is unaware of the personal approaches. While some churches are happy to go along with both methods, it would normally seem more ethical to go in either the front door (of corporate giving) or the back door (individual donors), rather than both. Because churches sometime budget support knowing of the congregational interest in a mission, they are left stranded when that support appears not to be forthcoming. Unaware of the private donations, they are sometimes forced to transfer funds from the general account in order to meet their obligations. When all the facts become know, a rift is created in the church/parachurch relationship.

Further, in this same connection, some Commission members are aware of businessmen who have turned completely against certain parachurch agencies because of ceaseless pressure—often by telephone—to give large amounts of money. Sometimes, professional fund-raisers raise more ire than funds, especially when common Christian courtesy and consideration are lacking in their approaches. When organizations get to learn that one man on a church board or budget committee was a fly in the ointment, they rarely realize the degree to which they may have brought it on themselves through previous high-pressure solicitation.

Some large Christian organizations confuse the Christian public (and especially church leaders) by allowing different levels of their network to function independently of one another. The Commission was told of one church that was approached for funds during the same year by local, national, and international entities of the same organization. The situation was further complicated because one of its members was also raising his own support as a local staff member of that same agency. We, therefore, urge organizations so constituted to ensure that the left hand *does* know what the right hand is doing; to recognize what is reasonable in appealing for funds; and to adopt a policy which will relieve the confusion in the minds of the supporting public.

Problems Which Can be Resolved by Those Giving and Receiving Overseas Aid

Concerns of the sending agencies about their home churches.

(a) Imbalance between evangelism and social responsibility

A whole generation has now gone by since evangelical leaders started seriously educating the Christian public on the need for the church to meet the needs of the *whole* man. Giant advances have been made. Many believe that the combined humanitarian activities of evangelicals around the world have already surpassed those of their liberal counterparts. So much has this been the case that a few evangelical leaders have expressed concern at what they see as a growing imbalance at the expense of evangelism. The Lausanne Covenant sought to emphasize the priorities with the words "In the Church's mission of sacrificial service, evangelism is primary."

Several denominations still appear to be suspicious of relief and development projects. These are reluctant to help, and often see their mission in the world as "witnessing" alone. Such groups do not encourage Christian relief agencies and, as far as possible, protect their people from being indoctrinated.

The Commission pleads with denominational educators who fall into this category to consider the possibility of initiating serious interaction with Christian social agencies which are sound in the faith and evangelistically active. This may well result in a healthier, more balanced Christian outlook. (Readers interested in this subject should obtain a copy of *Lausanne Occasional Paper No. 21—The Grand Rapids Report: Evangelism and Social Responsibility: An Evangelical Commitment.*)

(b) Uncritical acceptance of secular media reports

Christians sometimes appear to be more influenced by mass media reports and gossip than they are by the Scriptures and the actual facts of a situation. Staffs of respected relief agencies may be under attack by Christians whose suspicions about finances, once aroused, refuse to be put to rest. A segment of secular—and sometimes religious—journalism seems to take every opportunity to call into question the honesty, judgment, and integrity of relief agencies, especially in the sphere of administrative costs and how much of each dollar given actually reaches the hungry and the dispossessed. Doubtless, some agencies do exist where such criticism is justified. But many more are to be found with sound judgment, transparent honesty, and, what seems to us, reasonable administrative overhead.

Whereas the frequency and exaggerations of some of these reports do serve as a self-monitoring check on all Christian relief organizations, the Commission urges the Christian public—and especially pastors and leaders—to contact the agency in question and ask for the facts (such as a financial statement). An alternative route would be to contact monitoring agencies such as the Evangelical Council for Financial Accountability (in the U.S.A.), umbrella groups like the Canadian Council of Christian Charities (in Canada), or similar bodies in other countries. Once satisfactory answers are obtained, we would urge pastors to inform their flocks, encouraging their people to ignore incorrect media reports and to support the agency with prayer and loving help.

(c) Giving only the leftovers

Western materialistic living and the indulging in increased levels of luxury has sometimes resulted in those from the wealthier countries giving only from what is left over after necessities and luxuries have been bought. Staff of relief agencies are not alone in feeling we would all do well to heed the attitude of King David who rebuked the misguided generosity of Araunah, the Jebusite, with the penetrating words, "Neither will I offer to the Lord my God of that which costs me nothing" (2 Sam. 24:24).

The press occasionally reports a case of costly sacrifice in order to help others. The consequent amazement of the public serves to confirm our thinking that we must normally hardly notice the loss of monthly, or occasional, checks we write to relieve the needs of the world.

The Commission supports the embracing of a simpler life-style by those whose needs are more than met. History would teach us that wealthy nations which do not voluntarily change their ways to help the poor are often brought to their knees by times of economic chaos.

(d) Too much emphasis on buildings

A leader of one international relief agency believes that some churches' preoccupation with buildings is a major reason for a low level of concern for the hurting world. He sees this as particularly true in North America. Whereas few would underestimate the immense value of a suitable structure in which a church can meet, there is a very real sense in which four walls can be the greatest hindrance to fulfilling the real mission of the Church. This is not only because much of our evangelism is consequently aimed at "saints and seats," but because funds, otherwise available, are eaten away by expensive structures and crippling maintenance costs. The prototype of church life is unquestionably the Acts of the Apostles. Here we see the prime example of missions par excellence. The gospel was spread, the widows were looked after, and the needs of the saints in distant parts relieved. But those early Christians—as Christians—were not allowed to own buildings. Yet the Church never grew faster than it did in its first two hundred years, before the relaxing of the laws saw it eventually distracted from its primary purpose.

Recent information coming out of China would attest the wisdom of this pattern. In the first 30 years of Communist domination, little was heard about the Church. Some voiced the thoughts of thousands when they said, "We must assume the church in China is all but dead." The facts have now come to light and the opposite appears to be the case. While no official count is possible, it would seem that much that was dependent on Western help, denominational structures, and beautiful buildings disappeared, while the indigenous Church, reduced by social and political pressures to its basic cell structure, grew to an estimated 25–50 million people.

Jonathan Chao reports that in one county in Honan province, which had previously resisted Western missionary efforts, believers grew from four thousand in 1948 to 160,000 thirty-four years later. Writing in *Christianity Today* June 18, 1982, David Adeney points out that the Church was not only deprived of its buildings but is still "not allowed to support full-time workers—pastoral ministry has been carried on by church members who work during the day and give their time in the evenings to the work of the Lord. Leadership usually emerges from the church prayer meetings. Appointed by members of the church, the leaders are not responsible to any outside organization. They are self-governing, self-supporting, and self-propagating."

Whereas it would be naive to think that the restricting circumstances in which the Chinese Church thrived could be artificially imposed upon, or simulated in, the free and wealthy nations of the West, history provides ample evidence that a simpler organizational structure in the church not only facilitates multiplication, but also frees millions of dollars for feeding the hungry and relieving the distress of the world's poorer peoples.

The Commission can well understand why a church, virtually crippled under a heavy load of building debt, would bar its doors to independent and even denominational relief agencies. The guilt would be increased, by sensing what could have been accomplished if the congregation had not yielded to the desire for "the biggest church in town."

Eastminster Presbyterian Church in suburban Wichita, U.S.A., provides an example of a congregation which found a better way. The congregation had planned a $525,000 church building program for 1976. Then when an earthquake struck Guatemala in February of that year, the Wichita church learned that many evangelical congregations in the Central American nation had lost their buildings. An elder posed this question: "How can we set out to buy an ecclesiastical Cadillac when our brothers and sisters in Guatemala have lost their little Volkswagen?" The church slashed its building plans by two-thirds and borrowed $120,000 from the bank to rebuild 26 Guatemalan churches and 28 Guatemalan pastors' homes. The Wichita pastor reported that the congregation's action had "meant more to Eastminster Presbyterian than to Guatemala."

We all would do well to re-read the Acts of Apostles and reassess our priorities. While we do recognize the value of suitable buildings, we feel strongly that any church can easily be gripped by an "edifice complex" and, in the process, lose a vital concern for evangelism and missions.

*Concerns of the Churches of Receiving Countries About Sending
Agencies*

(a) Is the aid really needed?

Church leaders in countries receiving Western aid sometimes
question the factors which determine the selection of projects from the
large number of applications received by an agency. They feel they are
frequently not the most needy. Some nationals are all too aware of the
situations in the donor country which affect such decisions. "What type
of project will merit government matching grants?" may well determine whether the agency will eventually dig a well, start a reforesta-
tion program, or open a clinic in a needy rural area. Major crises which
make international headlines often attract dozens of relief agency
personnel to the scene, eager to rebuild anything which was destroyed
by earthquake or carried away by the tidal wave.

In most cases these are responses to urgent cries for help received
by the agencies, and the Commission expressed its thankfulness to God
that there are those called by him to this great work. Yet church leaders
in the hurting countries are frequently disturbed when they see other
personnel searching for projects which have even the most remote
connection with the crisis. They wonder why an equal amount of
money could not be designated for needs which, in national eyes, are
more urgently deserving. One reason, of course, is that the public tends
to give more generously to those crises publicized on television. Each
donor wants his money used for that, and that alone. As more and more
agencies arrive at the site, instead of thanking God that the needs have
been largely met, they find themselves bordering on panic for fear that
a project will not be found to meet the designated criteria of funds
flowing into the home office.

Such a scenario not only upsets the churches of the receiving
country but increases the competition between the uninvited agencies,
who become more determined to be first on the scene at the next
emergency. Is it, therefore, any wonder that the evangelistic activity,
often so effective in a time of crisis and upheaval, is done in a piecemeal
and disorganized way because of the strained relationships between
the churches and some of the agencies involved? The communicating
of the facts to sister churches in the donor country drives in the wedge
of suspicion still further.

The Commission recognizes the complexity of this problem, but
urges those parties involved in such international crises to sit down
together to find a solution which will not destroy the observed unity of
the Body of Christ in that country. We would also ask the Christian

public to be less demanding in the use of surplus funds, which may well be more effectively used by being re-designated to a lower-profile project.

(b) The danger of destroying self-identity

Some highly respected Third World church leaders have, for years now, been distressed over the destructive potential of foreign aid. Caution needs to be shown to ensure that self-reliance, self-esteem, or self-identity of the recipients not be destroyed. The churches of India have a saying, "You cannot walk with Western crutches," and together with leaders from African and other nations, have expressed their concerns to well-meaning but sometimes short-sighted Western relief groups. The concern has reached the point in many countries where it is actually becoming difficult to help at all. It is not that the needs have been met—they are as serious as ever. It is rather a case of national pride overruling the receiving of needed aid when it so destroys the selfhood of a people.

Most of the established agencies are, we believe, fully aware of this danger. With the increase of the number of groups involved in relief and development projects, the Commission recommends that associations which bring relief agencies together frequently discuss and, if possible, monitor these tendencies. We must strive together for partnership without paternalism.

(c) Recruitment of nationals

Organizations with designated funds but limited time sometimes have to disburse or distribute monies without opportunity to adequately check the credentials of intermediaries. National leaders, not consulted on a project, are occasionally horrified to hear of grants being used for undesignated purposes. Not infrequently, a project office is opened where members of the staff are all relatives of the trustee of the funds. While this may be acceptable in some cultures, leaders of most receiving countries and individual donors in the West see it as an unwise and opportunistic practice.

For many years, Third World church leaders have voiced their concern over the relatively high salaries paid to national workers by multinational Christian corporations. Such policies have a way of spoiling the workers and spawning an atmosphere of jealousy, greed, and dissatisfaction. This often results in inflationary budgeting with which smaller churches or organizations cannot cope. Furthermore, the thought of reward, rather than of privilege of serving God, takes over as the motivating factor for the one seeking Christian employment. The displeasure of national church leaders with this practice is unlikely to further cooperative evangelism. While we would not convey the suggestion that relief agency staff be paid less than church leaders, we do feel strongly that Western agencies have a moral obligation to consult both secular and church leaders to ensure their offers are not totally out of line.

(d) Life-style of Western personnel

The traveling life-style of some of today's parachurch leaders is hardly reflected in the well-known Christmas hymn:

> *Thou didst leave Thy throne and Thy kingly crown*
> *When Thou camest to earth for me,*
> *But in Bethlehem's home there was found no room*
> *For Thy holy nativity.*
> *The foxes found rest and the birds their nest*
> *In the shade of the forest tree,*
> *But Thy couch was the sod, O Thou Son of God*
> *In the deserts of Galilee.*

Such was the living standard of the Mission Leader par excellence. It becomes embarrassing to sing such words when our life-styles are in stark contrast to the community living in poverty around us. The Incarnation itself was the outstanding example of self-emptying in order to identify with men in their need. The birth, baptism, and death of the Lord Jesus on the cross were expressly for this purpose. The most elementary of mission principles teaches us that it is difficult to identify with a people we wish to reach, unless we are willing to adopt at least some of their customs and standards. This is not to suggest that we must dress in national costume, but it is to urge us to avoid that which offends the national conscience. Church leaders in developing countries are increasingly concerned about unnecessary, even luxurious, living standards of Western agency personnel, who often leave the impression of corporate wealth and material indulgence. While we recognize the wisdom of taking all necessary precautions in health and hygiene, there are, frequently, areas of our lives open to the public where it is not essential to live the way we sometimes do.

The Commission urges umbrella organizations (such as the Association of Evangelical Relief and Development Organizations— AERDO) to establish some self-monitoring checks to bring moral pressure on those whose overseas life-styles bring discredit on the gospel. A simpler living standard would not only reduce overhead but make the church in the receiving country more open to cooperative evangelism.

We also recommend that church leaders in developing countries, genuinely wanting to show the best side of their hospitality to visiting personnel, find ways other than reserving rooms for them in the most luxurious hotels. We should remember that experienced Westerners are very cognizant of the Eastern custom of accepting what is offered. They are, therefore, unlikely to ask for a last-minute change, lest they offend the host. Onlookers, seeing the class of their accommodation, have no way of knowing who is responsible.

(e) The ignoring of protocol

Time and again, Western missionaries or lone nationals (connected with a missionary agency or a national church) will request aid from interdenominational agencies in the West. Sometimes the projects are most worthwhile, and unsuspecting agencies may well agree to the funding. Later, the church or mission agency under which the applicant operates gets to hear of the project through a third party or by observing the development of the scheme *in situ*. Questions are asked and the funding agency becomes the scapegoat. The national church is indeed justified in wondering a) why the individual did not go through the right denominational channels and b) why the funding agency supplied the aid without consulting them. It is not unknown for the denomination to have turned down a previous application for the same project, not for lack of funds, but because the timing was wrong, or because it would affect other programs which were planned. Bad feeling results. The agency concerned is blacklisted. Cooperation in evangelism—or in anything else—is seriously jeopardized.

Larger, well-established organizations are well aware of the problems such actions can cause, and they do everything in their power to avoid them. Smaller, less-experienced agencies may, however, swallow the bait unsuspectingly, only to find themselves on the hot seat.

The Commission pleads with individual missionaries or national workers to observe protocol wherever possible, and encourages funding agencies to avoid unpleasant situations by double-checking before granting aid to this type of project.

Concerns of Sending Agencies About Churches in the Receiving Countries

Most Christian relief agencies prefer to channel funds for a requested project through Christian churches in recipient countries. Where this is not possible (or, sometimes, not desirable), other Christian groups or individual groups are sought out to act as intermediaries. Sheer logistics or a need for urgency may occasionally call for secular or government structures to be used.

Experienced agencies are, nevertheless, sometimes reluctant to entrust their funds or goods to Christian churches because of having had their fingers previously burned. The concerns most often mentioned are (a) the need for trustworthiness, (b) the need for efficiency, and (c) the need for financial accountability.

(a) The need for trustworthiness

Not a few funding agencies feel that the sub-Christian moral standards of some receiving countries are often tolerated in national churches and practiced by some of those handling relief funds. Churches previously acting as channels for aid have sometimes left much to be desired, by way of openness and honesty in their arrangements. Conscious of their role as stewards of the gifts of others, the funding agencies want to ensure that aid is received only by the people and projects for which it is designated. This does not always happen. Conflict of interest on the part of intermediaries sometimes results in diverted aid, or, at least favoritism towards certain people or districts. Past favors are even reciprocated at such opportune times. Furthermore, in addition to the "family only" policy of employment discussed above, some national churches, on seeing how much money is being poured into a project, begin to put pressure on the funding group for their cut of the funds, the requested percentage increasing each year. National churches who wonder why they have been dropped would do well to consider these facts.

(b) The need for efficiency

Christians are not always the most efficient intermediaries for relief funds. While national churches often feel slighted at being bypassed, many have still not learned to pay enough attention to preparing themselves for speedy and efficient handling of funds, food, or medical supplies. If church leaders of receiving countries would only be willing to discuss and resolve the concerns of the donor organizations, the latter may soon regain their eagerness to work with them. (A number of these concerns are included in the self-check test at the end of the section.)

(c) The need for financial accountability

The pressure is mounting—particularly in North America—for Christian humanitarian agencies to be more precisely accountable a) to their donors, b) to the press, and c) to the public in general. The mushrooming of relief agencies not properly equipped to raise and distribute funds brings increased accountability demands on other, well-established organizations. It is, therefore, to be expected that those on the receiving side of the aid will be required to give increasingly detailed accounting of the funds received. If churches in a Third World country wish to be channels, they must, now more than ever, a) demonstrate their ability to understand Christian principles of accounting, b) show a proven track record of having properly accounted for any aid which may have been previously channeled through them, and c) give reasonable evidence that they will keep good records and supply the necessary documents to the donor agency.

The Commission feels that the standards implicit in the above are not at all unreasonable, and that donor agencies are justified in expecting them to be met. We would, therefore, urge church leaders in developing countries to cooperate with these requirements so that aid can be speedily brought to the needy and a climate established in which cooperative evangelism can take place.

o o o

Self-Check Test No. 5
The Suspicion about Finances

For the consideration of pastors and church leaders

1. When did I last read a brief history of the Christian church?

2. Am I willing to acknowledge the significant contribution of voluntary agencies (a) where the church *could not* work and (b) where the church *was not* working?

3. Am I willing to take just five minutes right now to consider how a stranglehold by the institutionalized Church must ultimately destroy the initiative and effectiveness of important outreach groups?

4. Do I acknowledge that the church does have a responsibility to support valid and useful ministries outside its walls?

5. Do I realize that support for most parachurch groups must come almost in its entirety from church budgets or individual members of these churches?

6. Do I teach that our giving to God is never a "please offering" but a "thank offering" for all that he has done? Am I finding that this emphasis, apart from being a healthy one, is causing our people to give more in gratitude to God?

7. Do I suggest to the congregation that whereas their first responsibility is to the local church, they should allocate part of their tithe or some of their offerings for other Christian ministries?

8.   Am I content to allow our people to send their gifts *directly* to those ministries the church approves? (While the church budget will not reflect such giving, the time-saving for the treasurer will be significant.) If I don't like this idea, what am I trying to prove?

9.   Quite apart from individual giving to parachurch agencies, am I willing to suggest the church set a further example by giving a percentage of its corporate disbursements also?

10.   Do I really believe "it is more blessed to give than receive"? Am I then confidently expecting that God's blessing will accompany our recognizing the unity of the Body of Christ in this way?

11.   Am I willing to show the audited statement of our church finances to the local parachurch leader in the same way as I expect to see his?

For the consideration of parachurch leaders

1.   Am I in agreement with the principle of a potential or existing donor giving priority to his local church in the matter of tithes and offerings? Why?

2.   Are audited financial statements readily available for donors, church leaders, the press, or the leaders of other Christian agencies? If not, why not?

3.   Do my staff tug unwisely at the purse strings of a congregation they have been invited to address? Do I instruct them to discuss first with the pastor what would be in order?

4.   Which items in my program or ministry budgets may be looked upon by other Christian leaders as more appropriately slotted under administration, publicity, or fund-raising? With whom should I openly discuss this?

5.   Are all the travel, hotel, and restaurant expenses of my staff really essential? Are there instances where public transportation would be adequate and almost as convenient as more expensive means?

6.   If Jesus were incarnated in my body, doing my ministry, would he have basically the same life-style? What may be different? Am I willing to reevaluate and consider changing?

7.   Do we ever take unfair advantage of one-time givers to special projects, particularly where sponsorship of a child or young person is concerned? Do I feel it is right in every case to add the names to a general mailing list? Would most of these givers express surprise on receiving an ongoing mailing? Is my conscience easy about this? Do I get irritated when it is done to me?

8. When we organize a project where young people or children need to be "sponsored" (e. g., by the mile, or by the hour) what determines the selection of the project? Is it what will attract the most young people? Or what will be most fun? Or do we consider genuine help to the community and significant benefit to the young person? Do we have any scruples about children soliciting from their own church families, who feel forced to give rather than appear unspiritual?

9. Do we respect requests for deletion from our mailing list? Do we act as speedily as we can?

10. Do I have others check the impression that is conveyed by a newsletter I have written? Before sending it out? Am I eager to alter any statements which are distorted, exaggerated, or which sound more dramatic or alarming than really is the case?

11. Do we inculcate unscriptural expectations in our donors by offering some reward for their sending a donation? Is not the satisfaction of giving to God a sufficient incentive? If I keep up this policy, what will the next generation be taught to expect when they give to God?

12. Are my organizational goals such that there is a strong likelihood we will financially overcommit ourselves, and look to our constituents to bail us out of the crisis? Is this fair?

13. Do we give our supporters an opportunity to give input before we initiate major programs or projects? What would it take to stop us proceeding after announcing a program?

14. Do we seek to raise funds by way of both corporate and individual solicitations from the same church? Does the pastor know about it? From us? Or from others?

15. Do we sometimes exert pressure to give, to the point where people are concerned, or too embarrassed, to say no?

16. Do the different levels or departments of our organization solicit funds from the same people? Knowingly, or unknowingly? Is this confusing for the donor? What can I do to relieve the situation?

17. Would I give to another organization if I knew about it what I know about our own, regarding the receiving and spending of funds?

18. If my expense account had to be paid from my personal income, would I make any changes? Where could I make changes if there were no funds available?

19. Have I sensed an attitude of defensiveness within me as I have read the foregoing questions? If so, why? Am I inwardly critical of them because they are unscriptural, or because I am not willing to change my life-style?

For Home Churches

1.   Is our church balanced in its mission giving? Are we concerned about both witness and service, home and abroad? Would I consider doing a personal study in the New Testament on what mission really is? Could the mission chairman do it with me?

2.   Do I take the trouble to check on the facts when media reports criticize a Christian organization, discouraging the giving of our people? How do I handle my findings if they conflict with the media report?

3.   Do I, by precept and practice, encourage simpler life-styles among the congregation, so that we, as a church, can better help the needy of the world?

4.   Are mortgage and maintenance costs crippling our church in its ability to give to missions? Did the church grow just as fast before we had this building? What future decisions would best help the church to become more missions-oriented?

For Sending Agencies

1.   What was the original incentive for creating this ministry to the world's underprivileged, undernourished peoples? Was it transparent beyond question? Were there ulterior motives?

2.   Do we sometimes unfairly exploit crises which make international headlines, knowing that the public giving potential to such projects is excellent?

3.   Do we allow government matching grant policies to determine the type of project we support, rather than considering the views of the receiving country churches and using more biblical means of guidance?

4.   Ten years from now, is it likely that most of our projects will be shown to have moved a needy people forward in the ability to look after themselves? In which way will this be seen? Do we have projects which are exceptions? Why?

5.   Have we acted in any country in a way which has the potential to destroy the self-esteem of a needy people? Can I correct the situation? Am I planning to learn from the mistake?

6.   Have we been the means whereby one or more nationals have been undesirably influenced through having been linked as staff, intermediaries, or recipients of overseas aid? How can I avoid this in the future?

7. Does my life-style or the life-style of our staff contradict the principles for living exemplified by the lowly "Master Aid-Giver" himself? Am I planning to make changes?

8. Does my way of life offend the very people who are on the receiving end of our aid? How will this affect the reception of the Good News should the opportunity present itself?

9. Have we observed protocol in the considering and the giving of overseas aid? Did we purposely avoid certain channels? Why? Is the intermediary the most desirable person? For what reason? Could better representation have been secured with a mixed committee?

10. Are we handling too many projects to provide satisfactory supervision or monitoring? Are the problems which are caused by being spread too thin outweighing the benefits of the aid?

For Receiving Country Churches

1. Is there only a spirit of selfless service in our desire to be the vehicle for aid to the people of our country or community? Have we been honest with the donor agency?

2. Will the community be better off because *we* handled the goods or funds? Why?

3. Have we ever shown partiality in our stewardship of aid? Do we favor certain districts, ethnic groups, churches, or individuals? Are we willing to confess our need for transparent honesty in future arrangements?

4. Are we demanding an unfair—or even an increasing—share of the funds "for administrative purposes"? Are we "using" the donor agency to serve our own ends?

5. Are our people well trained and efficient in the distribution of goods or monies? Am I willing to eat humble pie by calling in another church leader or a secular specialist to give us help or advice? Have I done all I could have done to ensure wise stewardship?

6. Have I been diligent in reporting back to the donor agency? Have I properly accounted for my trusteeship of funds? Have I met *their* standards? Do I appreciate that they are also accountable to *their* donors?

7. Am I withholding my own views or advice from the donor agency on their way of doing things? If certain activities cast them in a bad light, or are not beneficial to our people, will I tell them, even though it may hurt temporarily—or even cost me my job?

Directory of Organizations

Introduction

The following pages provide a list and brief descriptions of organizations that "support indigenous ministries." The directory was a joint effort of the planning committee for the Consultation on Support of Indigenous Ministries (COSIM) and the Missions Advanced Research and Communications Center (MARC), a division of World Vision International. Entries are based on the responses to the MARC questionnaire for the *1998-2000 Mission Handbook* from organizations who also returned a supplemental COSIM questionnaire.

An analysis of the data provided by the directory reveals that of the 51 organizations listed (including one Canadian agency), 31 reported a total of just over 16,000 fully or partially supported non-USA personnel serving in their own or another overseas country. This is almost one-half the number of all fully supported long-term USA missions personnel overseas.

There are other national Christian workers besides the 16,000 reported who benefit from the partner relationships of the reporting organizations. Some organizations, due to the nature of their programs, did not report specific numbers. For example, the Overseas Council for Theological Education and Missions did not report the number of non-USA personnel associated with their overseas programs. Although the ministry assists some 60 educational institutions worldwide, the staff and faculty of those schools are not necessarily individually supported and therefore were not reported on the organization's questionnaire.

In financial terms, the 51 organizations reported a combined total of just over $55 million annual income for overseas ministries. These organizations also support more than 500 long-term mission personnel or short-termers serving at least one year. Applying a factor to the organizations reporting the largest numbers of USA personnel suggests an estimated total support for national workers at about $40 million from these 51 organizations. Although this is a relatively small percentage of the more than $2 billion total North American missions giving, it is a significant annual investment for this growing movement.

Some Notes about the Directory

The brief descriptive paragraph for each organization is based on the denominational orientation and primary activities information supplied by the organization. It has the same general order for each agency so the reader is presented with a consistent descriptive format for each organization. Additional specific information, such as a merger, may also be included.

The survey invited organizations to include their board-adopted short purpose or mission statement with their filled-out questionnaire. This is the portion of the description enclosed in quotes. Some of the statements are concise and shown in their entirety. For most, however, such common or similar phrases as "exists for the purpose of" are replaced by ellipses to have a more concise statement.

The category of nonresidential mission personnel are "persons not residing in the country or countries of their ministry but traveling overseas at least 12 weeks per year on operational aspects of the ministry."

In the "countries" section, a number sometimes follows the name of the country. This is the number of fully-supported USA personnel serving in that country.

John Siewert, MARC
World Vision International

Directory of Organizations

ACTS International Ministries

(719)282-1247   Fax: (719)282-1139

E-Mail: 73524.1100@compuserve.com

P.O. Box 62725, Colorado Springs, CO 80962

Dr. Alvin Low, President

    A transdenominational support agency of evangelical tradition engaged in training, leadership development, and national churches support.

    ".. equipping national Christian leaders in the least evangelized, economically deprived, and restricted countries of the world..."

Year Founded in USA   1991

Income for Overseas Ministries $ 40,000

Fully Supported USA Personnel Overseas:

Nonresidential mission personnel   1

Other Personnel:

Home ministry & office staff in USA   1

◆ ◆ ◆ ◆ ◆

Advancing Indigenous Missions

(210)367-3513   Fax: (210)734-7620

P.O. Box 690042, San Antonio, TX 78269

James W. Colley, Exec. Director

    A transdenominational support agency of evangelical and charismatic tradition engaged in support of national missions and workers.

    "..to mobilize Christian churches, organizations, and individuals for prayer, financial, and logistical support of indigenous missions."

Year Founded in USA   1990

Income for Overseas Ministries $ 9,124

Personnel:

Home ministry & office staff in USA   1

Advancing Native Missions

(804)293-8829   Fax: (804)293-7586

E-Mail: ANM@adnamis.org

Web: http://www.cstone.net/~adnamis/

P.O. Box 5036, Charlottesville, VA 22905

Carl A. Gordon, President

A transdenominational support agency of evangelical tradition engaged in support of national missions, Bible distribution, funds transmission, leadership development, and mission-related research. Includes 1995 merger of GlobaLink Ministries, Inc.

".. to seek out, evaluate, and support native missions groups .. who are working among unreached people groups..."

Year Founded in USA	1990
Income for Overseas Ministries	$ 1,400,000
Fully Supported USA Personnel Overseas:	
Expecting to serve more than 4 years	6
Other Personnel:	
Non USA serving in own/other country	6
Short-Term less than 1 year from USA	40
Home ministry & office staff in USA	14

Countries: Asia-Gen 5, Indonesia 1.

◆ ◆ ◆ ◆ ◆

Ambassadors for Christ Intl.

(770)980-2020   **Fax: (980)956-8144**

E-Mail: 73440.127@compuserve.com

1355 Terrell Mill Rd. #1484, Marietta, GA 30067

Rev. Allan Gardner, Intl. Director

A nondenominational support agency of evangelical tradition engaged in funds transmission for national worker training and evangelism.

"..to help fulfill the Great Commission through support of national preaching ministries."

Year Founded in USA	1972
Income for Overseas Ministries	$ 624,747
Personnel:	
Non USA serving in own/other country	119
Home ministry & office staff in USA	6

Countries: Dominica, Egypt, Fiji, Ghana, Guadeloupe, India, Indonesia, Kenya, Myanmar/Burma, Nigeria, Pakistan, Philippines, S Africa, Singapore, Spain, St Vincent, Sudan, Tonga, UK, Zambia.

Anglican Orthodox Church

(704)873-8365   **Fax: (704)873-8948**

P.O. Box 128, Statesville, NC 28687

Bishop Robert J. Godfrey, Exec. Officer

A denominational support agency of Anglican tradition engaged in support of national church workers, Christian education, and evangelism.

Year Founded in USA   1963
Income for Overseas Ministries   NR
Personnel:
    Non USA serving in own/other country   11
    Home ministry & office staff in USA   6
Countries: Fiji, India, Japan, Kenya, Liberia, Madagascar, Pakistan, Philippines.

Asian Outreach U.S.A.
(714)557-9160   Fax: **(714)557-2742**
E-Mail: JR2135@aol.com
3941 S. Bristol St. #67, Santa Ana, CA 92704
Rev. James R. Swanson, Exec. Director
    An interdenominational support agency of evangelical tradition engaged in literature distribution, Bible distribution, broadcasting, literature production, and support of national churches.

Year Founded in USA   1960
Income for Overseas Ministries $ 1,078,000
Amount of Gifts-In-Kind $ 1,000,000
Fully Supported USA Personnel Overseas:
    Expecting to serve more than 4 years   1
    Expecting to serve 1 up to 4 years   5
Other Personnel:
    Non USA serving in own/other country   3
    Short-Term less than 1 year from USA   8
    Home ministry & office staff in USA   1
Countries: Asia-Gen 2, Hong Kong 3, Japan 1, Mongolia.

Barnabas International
(815)395-1335   Fax: **(815)395-1385**
E-Mail: 75453.2463@compuserve.com
P.O. Box 11211, Rockford, IL 61126
Dr. Lareau Lindquist, Exec. Director
    A nondenominational sending agency of evangelical tradition engaged in missionary pastoral care, leadership development, support of national churches, and psychological counseling.

".. to edify, enrich, encourage, and strengthen [missionaries, pastors, national church leaders and their families] ... through personal, small group, and conference ministries."

Year Founded in USA 1986
Income for Overseas Ministries $ 330,830
Fully Supported USA Personnel Overseas:
  Expecting to serve more than 4 years 4
  Nonresidential mission personnel 12
Other Personnel:
  Short-Term less than 1 year from USA 7
  Home ministry & office staff in USA 2
Countries: Philippines 2, Ukraine 2.

Bright Hope International
(847)526-5566 **Fax: (847)526-0073**
E-Mail: BrightHope@aol.com
1000 Brown Street #207, Wauconda, IL 60084
Mr. Craig H. Dyer, President
  A nondenominational service agency of evangelical tradition engaged in development including alternative trade organizations and jobs, Bible distribution, support of national workers, and relief aid.

Year Founded in USA 1968
Income for Overseas Ministries $ 276,973
Personnel:
  Non USA serving in own/other country 53
  Short-Term less than 1 year from USA 4
  Home ministry & office staff in USA 7
Countries: China (PRC), Guatemala, Kenya, Romania, Russia, Uzbekistan, Vietnam, Yugoslavia.

China Ministries International
(818)398-0145 **Fax: (818)398-2361**
E-Mail: 104435.2547@compuserve.com
P.O. Box 40489, Pasadena, CA 91104
Rev. Ronald Yu, U.S. Director
Dr. Jonathan Chao, Founder and President
  A nondenominational support agency of evangelical and Reformed tradition engaged in theological education, Bible distribution, funds

transmission, leadership development, mission-related research, and missionary training.

".. for the evangelization of China, the strengthening of the Chinese Church .. by engaging in ministries of research, training of workers, and sending them to the harvest field..."

Year Founded in USA	1987
Income for Overseas Ministries	$ 440,000
Fully Supported USA Personnel Overseas:	
Expecting to serve more than 4 years	2
Expecting to serve 1 up to 4 years	1
Nonresidential mission personnel	1
Other Personnel:	
Non USA serving in own/other country	50
Home ministry & office staff in USA	3

Countries: Australia, Hong Kong 1, Korea-S, Philippines, Taiwan (ROC) 2, UK.

Christ for India, Inc.
(972)771-7221   Fax: (972)771-4021
P.O. Box 271086, Dallas, TX 75227
Dr. P. J. Titus, Founder/President
Arlene Phelps, Admin. Secretary

A nondenominational service agency of charismatic tradition engaged in church planting, training, corres. courses, evangelism, literature distribution, and support of national workers.

"... to 'make ready a people, prepared for the coming of the Lord'."

Year Founded in USA	1981
Income for Overseas Ministries	$ 187,254
Personnel:	
Non USA serving in own/other country	500
Short-Term less than 1 year from USA	30
Home ministry & office staff in USA	1

Countries: India.

Christ for the City International
(402)592-8332
E-Mail: InfoCFC@aol.com
P.O. Box 241827, Omaha, NE 68124
J. Paul Landrey, President

A transdenominational sending agency of evangelical tradition engaged in evangelism, church planting, childrens programs, leadership development, short-term programs coordination.

"To multiply 'open churches' in strategic population centers and inspire, equip and encourage every believer in these 'open churches' to influence their world for Christ."

Year Founded in USA	1995
Income for Overseas Ministries	$ 1,912,372
Fully Supported USA Personnel Overseas:	
Expecting to serve more than 4 years	31
Expecting to serve 1 up to 4 years	16
Other Personnel:	
Non USA serving in own/other country	60
Bi-Vocational/Tentmakers from USA	8
Short-Term less than 1 year from USA	645
Home ministry & office staff in USA	7

Countries: Argentina 2, Brazil 2, Colombia 8, Costa Rica 18, Mexico 14, Peru 1, Spain 2, Switzerland.

◆ ◆ ◆ ◆ ◆

Christ for the Island World
(910)855-0656   **Fax: (910)854-1555**
P.O. Box 18962, Greensboro, NC 27419
Rev. Ken Taylor, President

An interdenominational support agency of evangelical tradition engaged in support of national workers, church planting, and evangelism.

Year Founded in USA	1983
Income for Overseas Ministries	$ 50,000
Personnel:	
Non USA serving in own/other country	111
Home ministry & office staff in USA	2

Countries: Brazil, Indonesia, Russia.

◆ ◆ ◆ ◆ ◆

Christian Aid Mission
(804)977-5650   **Fax: (804)295-6814**
E-Mail: CAidInfo@christianaid.org
Web: http://www.christianaid.org/
3045 Ivy Rd., Charlottesville, VA 22903
Dr. Robert V. Finley, Chairman

A nondenominational service agency of evangelical tradition raising
financial support for indigenous mission boards and Bible institutes
involved in church planting, evangelism, literature distribution, and
missionary training.

"Seeks out and evaluates indigenous mission groups effectively reaching
unreached people groups . Sends help .. for support .. training and sending
out of new missionaries .."

Year Founded in USA	1953
Income for Overseas Ministries	$ 3,663,916
Fully Supported USA Personnel Overseas:	
Nonresidential mission personnel	8
Other Personnel:	
Non USA serving in own/other country	2,338
Home ministry & office staff in USA	20

Countries: Albania, Argentina, Armenia, Bangladesh, Bolivia, Brazil, Cambodia,
China (PRC), Colombia, Costa Rica, Croatia, Cuba, Dominican Rep, Egypt, Gambia,
Ghana, Guatemala, Haiti, Honduras, India, Indonesia, Jordan, Kazakhstan, Kenya,
Kyrgyzstan, Laos, Macedonia, Malawi, Mexico, Mongolia, Myanmar/Burma, Nepal,
Nigeria, Pakistan, Papua New Guin, Paraguay, Peru, Philippines, Poland, Romania,
Russia, Rwanda, S Africa, Sierra Leone, Sri Lanka, Syria, Tajikistan, Tanzania,
Thailand, Tibet, Turkey, Uganda, Ukraine, Uruguay, Uzbekistan, Vietnam, West Bank,
Zimbabwe.

◆ ◆ ◆ ◆ ◆

Christian Dynamics
(602)878-6892
10878 N. 57th Ave., Glendale, AZ 85304
Dr. Harvey M. Lifsey, President

A transdenominational service agency of evangelical tradition engaged
in support of national workers, orphanage work, corres. courses,
evangelism, and literacy work.

".. to support national workers who will penetrate with the Gospel into
unreached areas and establish indigenous churches."

Year Founded in USA	1976
Income for Overseas Ministries	$ 100,000
Amount of Gifts-In-Kind	$ 90,000
Fully Supported USA Personnel Overseas:	
Nonresidential mission personnel	1
Other Personnel:	
Non USA serving in own/other country	48
Nonresidential personnel partially supported	1

Short-Term less than 1 year from USA 2
Home ministry & office staff in USA 1
Countries: Cambodia, India.

◆ ◆ ◆ ◆ ◆

Christian Information Service, Inc. Missions Division
(804)973-8439 **Fax: (804)973-7470**
P.O. Box 6511, Charlottesville, VA 22906
William T. Bray, President
  A transdenominational support agency of evangelical tradition engaged in services for other agencies, and mobilization for mission.
Year Founded in USA 1972
Income for Overseas Ministries $ 45,890
Fully Supported USA Personnel Overseas:
Nonresidential mission personnel 2
Other Personnel:
Short-Term less than 1 year from USA 10
Home ministry & office staff in USA 2

◆ ◆ ◆ ◆ ◆

Christian Outreach International
(561)778-0571 **Fax: (561)778-6781**
E-Mail: COIhq@sprynet.com
P.O. Box 2823, Vero Beach, FL 32961
Mr. Jack Isleib, Exec. Director
  An interdenominational service agency of evangelical tradition engaged in short-term programs coordination, evangelism, support of national workers, and mobilization for mission.
Year Founded in USA 1984
Income for Overseas Ministries $ 1,400,000
Fully Supported USA Personnel Overseas:
Expecting to serve more than 4 years 1
Expecting to serve 1 up to 4 years 26
Other Personnel:
Non USA serving in own/other country 11
Short-Term less than 1 year from USA 500
Home ministry & office staff in USA 12
Countries: Czech Rep 7, France 1, Ukraine 9, Venezuela 10.

◆ ◆ ◆ ◆ ◆

David Livingstone Missionary Foundation
(918)494-9902   Fax: (918)496-2873
E-Mail: 103460.3661@compuserve.com
P.O. Box 232, Tulsa, OK 74102
Mr. Lonnie Rex, President
A nondenominational service agency of independent tradition engaged in support of national workers.

Year Founded in USA	1969
Income for Overseas Ministries	$ 1,948,100
Amount of Gifts-In-Kind	$ 755,000
Fully Supported USA Personnel Overseas:	
Nonresidential mission personnel	1
Other Personnel:	
Home ministry & office staff in USA	7

◆ ◆ ◆ ◆ ◆

Eastern European Bible Mission
(719)577-4450   Fax: (719)577-4453
P.O. Box 110, Colorado Springs, CO 80901
Mr. Hank Paulson, Founder & President
A nondenominational support agency of evangelical tradition engaged in youth and programs, evangelism, and literature distribution through support of national workers.

Year Founded in USA	1972
Income for Overseas Ministries	$ 484,000
Fully Supported USA Personnel Overseas:	
Nonresidential mission personnel	1
Other Personnel:	
Non USA serving in own/other country	69
Short-Term less than 1 year from USA	60
Home ministry & office staff in USA	6

Countries: Czech Rep, Hungary, Romania, Slovakia, Ukraine.

◆ ◆ ◆ ◆ ◆

Equipping the Saints
(540)234-6222
E-Mail: ETS@rica.net
1254 Keezletown Road, Weyers Cave, VA 24486
Rev. Keith A. Jones, Exec. Director

A nondenominational service agency of evangelical tradition engaged in purchasing services and supplying equipment.

"..to enhance the outreach of indigenous evangelical ministries .. by providing appropriate human, material and financial resources."

Year Founded in USA	1991
Income for Overseas Ministries	$ 24,000
Amount of Gifts-In-Kind	$ 22,000
Personnel:	
Home ministry & office staff in USA	4

◆ ◆ ◆ ◆ ◆

Eurovangelism
(905)821-6301   Fax: (905)821-6311
E-Mail: ETS@rica.net
207-2476 Argentia Rd., Missisauga, ON L5N 6M1, Canada
Mr. John Murray, Exec. Director

A nondenominational agency of evangelical tradition supporting national workers and churches, TEE, evangelism, and relief aid.

"..to serve the church across Europe by envisioning, encouraging, and equipping national Christian workers."

Year Founded in Canada	1991
Income for Overseas Ministries	$ 24,000
Amount of Gifts-In-Kind	$ 22,000
Personnel:	
Home ministry & office staff in USA	4

◆ ◆ ◆ ◆ ◆

Every Home for Christ
(719)260-8888   Fax: (719)260-7408
E-Mail: Wes@ehc.org
P.O. Box 35930, Colorado Springs, CO 80935
Dr. Dick Eastman, President
Rev. Wesley R. Wilson, VP Intl. Administration

A transdenominational service agency of evangelical tradition engaged in literature distribution/production, church planting, evangelism, and support of national churches.

".. to serve, mobilize and train the Church to pray and actively participate in the systematic personal presentation of a printed or repeatable message of the Gospel of Jesus Christ to every home in the whole world..."

Year Founded in USA	1946

Income for Overseas Ministries	$ 5,369,897

Personnel:

Non USA serving in own/other country	1,124
Nonresidential personnel partially supported	1
Short-Term less than 1 year from USA	4
Home ministry & office staff in USA	55

Countries: Africa-Gen, Albania, Argentina, Asia-Gen, Bangladesh, Belarus, Benin, Bolivia, Brazil, Bulgaria, Burkina Faso, CIS-Gen, Cambodia, China (PRC), Congo, Congo/Zaire, Costa Rica, Cote d'Ivoire, Cuba, Czech Rep, El Salvador, Equat Guinea, Estonia, Ethiopia, Europe-Gen, France, Ghana, Greece, Guatemala, Honduras, India, Indonesia, Italy, Kazakhstan, Korea-S, Kyrgyzstan, Latin Am-Gen, Lebanon, Malawi, Malaysia, Mexico, Mozambique, Myanmar/Burma, Namibia, Nepal, Nicaragua, Nigeria, Oceania-Gen, Panama, Papua New Guin, Paraguay, Peru, Philippines, Poland, Russia, Sierra Leone, Solomon Isls, Spain, Sri Lanka, Tajikistan, Thailand, Togo, Turkmenistan, Ukraine, Uruguay, Uzbekistan, Zambia, Zimbabwe.

◆ ◆ ◆ ◆ ◆

Friendship Ministries
(206)823-1405
Totem Lake P.O. Box 8387, Kirkland, WA 98034

Denise C. Johnson, President & Founder

An interdenominational support agency of evangelical and ecumenical tradition engaged in support of national churches, Christian education, and psychological counseling.

".. to access and mobilize resources for the support of mission teams and to establish, encourage and develop friendships to answer and meet the needs in the Eastern European Church."

Year Founded in USA	1988
Income for Overseas Ministries	$ 15,000

Fully Supported USA Personnel Overseas:

Expecting to serve 1 up to 4 years	2

Other Personnel:

Bi-Vocational/Tentmakers from USA	2
Short-Term less than 1 year from USA	2

Countries: Poland 2.

◆ ◆ ◆ ◆ ◆

GlobaLink Ministries, Inc.
See: Advancing Native Missions

◆ ◆ ◆ ◆ ◆

Gospel for Asia

(972)416-0340   **Fax: (972)416-6131**

E-Mail: info@gfa.org

Web: http://www.gfa.org

1932 Walnut Plaza, Carrollton, TX 75006

Rev. K. P. Yohannan, President

A nondenominational service agency of evangelical tradition engaged in missionary training, evangelism, broadcasting, church planting, leadership development, and support of natl. workers.

Year Founded in USA	1979
Income for Overseas Ministries	$ 5,901,816
Fully Supported USA Personnel Overseas:	
Nonresidential mission personnel	2
Other Personnel:	
Non USA serving in own/other country	6,439
Short-Term less than 1 year from USA	28
Home ministry & office staff in USA	27

Countries: Bhutan, China (PRC), India, Myanmar/Burma, Nepal, Pakistan, Philippines, Russia, Sri Lanka, Thailand, Vietnam.

◆ ◆ ◆ ◆ ◆

Gospel Outreach Ministries Intl.

(314)789-2160   **Fax: (314)789-2789**

4478 Goldman Spur Rd., Hillsboro, MO 63050

Dr. Sam Paul Gokanakonda, Founder/CEO

A nondenominational support agency of charismatic and evangelical tradition engaged in evangelism, church planting, support of national workers, and mission-related research.

Year Founded in USA	1988
Income for Overseas Ministries	$ 91,704
Fully Supported USA Personnel Overseas:	
Nonresidential mission personnel	1
Other Personnel:	
Non USA serving in own/other country	250
Nonresidential personnel partially supported	1
Short-Term less than 1 year from USA	6
Home ministry & office staff in USA	3

Countries: India.

◆ ◆ ◆ ◆ ◆

Help for Christian Nationals, Inc.
(972)780-5909
P.O. Box 381006, Duncanville, TX 75137
Dr. John Jauchen, Director
   A transdenominational sending agency of evangelical tradition engaged in leadership development, extension education, literature distribution, support of national churches and workers, and training.
   ".. serving Christian national workers through economic and educational assistance, equipping them to be more effective in reaching their own people for Jesus Christ."

Year Founded in USA	1982
Income for Overseas Ministries	$ 225,000
Fully Supported USA Personnel Overseas:	
Expecting to serve more than 4 years	1
Nonresidential mission personnel	1
Other Personnel:	
Non USA serving in own/other country	9
Home ministry & office staff in USA	1

Countries: Guatemala, Honduras, India, Philippines, Russia, Spain 1.

◆ ◆ ◆ ◆ ◆

Hinduism International Ministries
(847)872-7022   Fax: (847)872-7022
E-Mail: Singhal@cs.uwp.edu
P.O. Box 602, Zion, IL 60099
Dr. Mahendra P. Singhal, Chairman
   A nondenominational support agency of independent tradition engaged in evangelism, leadership development, and training. Financial information from 1992 report.

Year Founded in USA	1986
Income for Overseas Ministries	$ 7,500
Personnel:	
Nonresidential personnel partially supported	6
Short-Term less than 1 year from USA	20
Home ministry & office staff in USA	2

◆ ◆ ◆ ◆ ◆

In Touch Mission International

(602)968-4100   Fax: (602)968-5462

E-Mail: 75222.2215@compuserve.com

P.O. Box 28240, Tempe, AZ 85285

Bill Bathman, Director

An interdenominational sending agency of Baptist tradition engaged in support of national workers, Bible distribution, evangelism, and providing medical supplies.

Year Founded in USA	1981
Income for Overseas Ministries	$ 151,000
Fully Supported USA Personnel Overseas:	
Expecting to serve more than 4 years	2
Other Personnel:	
Non USA serving in own/other country	7
Home ministry & office staff in USA	4

Countries: Europe-E 2, Mexico.

◆ ◆ ◆ ◆ ◆

India Gospel Outreach

(909)948-2404   Fax: (909)948-2406

E-Mail: 103417.3401@compuserve.com

Web: http://igo.ncsa.com/igo/

P.O. Box 550, Rancho Cucamonga, CA 91729

Rev. T. Valson Abraham, Founder/Director

A transdenominational service agency of charismatic and evangelical tradition partnering with national churches and workers in India engaged in church planting, theological education, evangelism, and leadership development.

".. planting dynamic churches in all 3,000 castes and tribes .. and establishing Bible training centers in all states of India .. by the year 2000."

Year Founded in USA	1984
Income for Overseas Ministries	$ 360,000
Personnel:	
Short-Term less than 1 year from USA	8
Home ministry & office staff in USA	7

Countries: India.

◆ ◆ ◆ ◆ ◆

India National Inland Mission
(818)241-4010
P.O. Box 652, Verdugo City, CA 91046
Mr. Paul C. Nelson, Treasurer
A nondenominational support agency of evangelical tradition engaged in funds transmission, church planting, childcare/orphanage programs, theological education, and literature distribution through partners in India.
Year Founded in USA   1964
Income for Overseas Ministries $ 768,989
Countries: India.

India Rural Evangelical Fellowship
(847)680-6767
E-Mail: IREF4US@aol.com
P.O. Box 1332, Park Ridge, IL 60068
Mr. Emmanuel Rebba, President
An interdenominational agency of evangelical tradition supporting national churches involved in church planting, orphanage/schools programs, Christian education, and evangelism.
Year Founded in USA   1985
Income for Overseas Ministries $ 290,220
Personnel:
Non USA serving in own/other country   127
Home ministry & office staff in USA   1
Countries: India.

International Cooperating Ministries
(757)827-6704   Fax: (757)838-6486
606 Aberdeen Rd., Hampton, VA 23661
Dois I. Rosser, Jr., Chairman
An interdenominational support agency of evangelical tradition engaged in church construction, broadcasting, and literature distribution/production through national workers.
"To encourage the growth of the national indigenous church without making that church dependent on outside resources..."
Year Founded in USA   1987
Income for Overseas Ministries $ 947,000

Personnel:

Home ministry & office staff in USA   5

♦ ♦ ♦ ♦ ♦

International Needs - USA
(360)354-1991   **Fax: (360)354-1991**
E-Mail: dculin@aol.com
P.O. Box 977, Lynden, WA 98264
Mr. David Culross, Exec. Director

A transdenominational service agency of evangelical tradition engaged
in support of national workers, childcare/orphanage programs, evangelism,
leadership development, and literature distribution.

Year Founded in USA   1975
Income for Overseas Ministries $ 512,298
Personnel:

Non USA serving in own/other country   402
Short-Term less than 1 year from USA   28
Home ministry & office staff in USA   8

Countries: Africa-Gen, Bangladesh, Colombia, Croatia, Czech Rep, Eritrea, Fiji,
Ghana, Hong Kong, India, Indonesia, Nepal, Philippines, Romania, Slovakia, Sri
Lanka, Uganda, Zambia.

International Partnership Ministries, Inc.
(717)637-7388   **Fax: (717)637-1618**
E-Mail: IPM@sun-link.com
P.O. Box 41, Hanover, PA 17331
Dr. Timothy B. Shorb, President

A nondenominational agency of Baptist tradition supporting, in
partnership with Two-Thirds World mission agencies, national workers
involved in leadership development.

Year Founded in USA   1982
Income for Overseas Ministries $ 520,532
Fully Supported USA Personnel Overseas:

Expecting to serve more than 4 years   2

Other Personnel:

Non USA serving in own/other country   89
Short-Term less than 1 year from USA   15

Home ministry & office staff in USA   4
Countries: Chile, Ghana, Haiti, India, Mexico, Paraguay, Togo 2.

Latin America Mission
(305)884-8400   **Fax: (305)885-8649**
E-Mail: info@lam.org
Web: http://www.lam.org
P.O. Box 52-7900, Miami, FL 33152
Dr. David M. Howard, President
    An interdenominational sending agency of evangelical tradition engaged in evangelism, church planting, theological education, leadership development, and literature distribution.
    ".. to encourage, assist and participate with the Latin church in the task of building the church of Jesus Christ in the Latin world and beyond."
Year Founded in USA   1921
Income for Overseas Ministries $ 4,299,335
Fully Supported USA Personnel Overseas:
    Expecting to serve more than 4 years   91
    Expecting to serve 1 up to 4 years   46
Other Personnel:
    Non USA serving in own/other country   39
    Short-Term less than 1 year from USA   58
    Home ministry & office staff in USA   28
Countries: Argentina 6, Bolivia 1, Brazil 2, Colombia 13, Costa Rica 73, Ecuador 1, Guatemala 2, Mexico 27, Panama, Peru 2, Spain 4, Venezuela 6.

◆ ◆ ◆ ◆ ◆

Mission 21 India
(616)453-8855   **Fax: (616)791-9926**
E-Mail: M21India@alliance.net
P.O. Box 141312, Grand Rapids, MI 49514
Rev. John F. DeVries, President
    An interdenominational support agency of evangelical tradition partnering with national organizations engaged in church planting, Bible distribution, childrens programs, development, literature distribution, and literacy work.
    "...to motivate, train, and assist national Indian denominations and missions to plant one new house church for every 1,000 persons."

Year Founded in USA	1990
Income for Overseas Ministries	$ 1,704,392
Amount of Gifts-In-Kind	$ 203,866
Fully Supported USA Personnel Overseas:	
Nonresidential mission personnel	1
Other Personnel:	
Home ministry & office staff in USA	13
Countries: India.	

◆ ◆ ◆ ◆ ◆

Mission O.N.E., Inc.

(615)672-9504   **Fax: (615)672-9513**

E-Mail: MissionWun@aol.com

P.O. Box 70, White House, TN 37188

Bob Schlinder, President

An interdenominational support agency of Baptist and evangelical tradition engaged in training and support of national workers for evangelism and church planting.

".. to mobilize the Church for the support of national missionaries, primarily among unreached people groups in developing nations."

Year Founded in USA	1991
Income for Overseas Ministries	$ 74,781
Personnel:	
Non USA serving in own/other country	151
Short-Term less than 1 year from USA	10
Home ministry & office staff in USA	3

Countries: China (PRC), Ethiopia, India, Indonesia, Kenya, Laos, Myanmar/Burma, Nepal, Pakistan, Sudan, Thailand, Uganda, Zambia.

◆ ◆ ◆ ◆ ◆

Mustard Seed, Inc.

(818)791-5123   **Fax: (818)398-2392**

E-Mail: mseedinc@wavenet.com

P.O. Box 400, Pasadena, CA 91114

Rev. Garry O. Parker, President

An interdenominational support agency of evangelical tradition partnering with churches and ministries engaged in Christian education, agricultural programs, church planting, childcare programs, medical work, and relief aid.

"... to assist in the task of world evangelization by means of compassionate services and verbal witness among tribal peoples, particularly those having to learn to cope with modernity..."

Year Founded in USA	1948
Income for Overseas Ministries	$ 795,298

Fully Supported USA Personnel Overseas:

Expecting to serve 1 up to 4 years	1

Other Personnel:

Non USA serving in own/other country	320
Short-Term less than 1 year from USA	1
Home ministry & office staff in USA	7

Countries: Indonesia, Papua New Guin 1, Taiwan (ROC).

◆ ◆ ◆ ◆ ◆

National Baptist Convention of America, Foreign Mission Board

(214)942-3311   Fax: **(214)943-4924**
P.O. Box 223665, Dallas, TX 75222
Rev. N. Andrew Allen, Exec. Director

A denominational support agency of Baptist tradition engaged in evangelism, church construction, Christian education, funds transmission, and support of national workers.

Year Founded in USA	1915
Income for Overseas Ministries	$ 390,000

Personnel:

Home ministry & office staff in USA	4

Countries: Ghana, Haiti, Jamaica.

◆ ◆ ◆ ◆ ◆

Overseas Council for Theological Education & Missions, Inc.

(317)788-7250   Fax: **(317)788-7257**
E-Mail: 76517.2770@compuserve.com
P.O. Box 17368, Indianapolis, IN 46217
Dr. John C. Bennett, President

A transdenominational support agency of evangelical tradition engaged in leadership development, theological education, TEE, funds transmission, and mission-related research in 15 key regions of the Two-Thirds World.

"... helping national seminaries and Bible colleges train their own people to become evangelists, teachers, pastors and missionaries..."

Year Founded in USA   1974
Income for Overseas Ministries $ 1,770,571
Fully Supported USA Personnel Overseas:
Nonresidential mission personnel   2
Other Personnel:
Home ministry & office staff in USA   18

◆ ◆ ◆ ◆ ◆

Partners in Asian Missions
(205)854-8418   Fax: (205)879-2407
E-Mail: JFSharpe@bham.mindspring.com
Web: http://www.mindspring.com/~jfsharpe
P.O. Box 531011, Birmingham, AL 35253
Rev. Jerry F. Sharpe, Intl. Director
        A nondenominational support agency of evangelical tradition engaged in leadership development, evangelism, and national worker support.
        ".. establishes strategic-level alliances with key regional leaders in order to develop cooperative projects and share evangelism training materials."
Year Founded in USA   1972
Income for Overseas Ministries $ 60,000
Fully Supported USA Personnel Overseas:
Nonresidential mission personnel   1
Other Personnel:
Non USA serving in own/other country   50
Countries: Asia-Gen.

◆ ◆ ◆ ◆ ◆

Partners International
(408)453-3800   Fax: (408)437-9708
E-Mail: chuckb@partnersintl.org
Web: http://www.partnersintl.org
P.O. Box 15025, San Jose, CA 95115-0025
Mr. Chuck Bennett, President
        A nondenominational support agency of evangelical tradition engaged in support of national workers, church planting, leadership development, management and consulting/training.
        "We link you with effective grass-roots Christian ministries worldwide."
Year Founded in USA   1943
Income for Overseas Ministries $ 8,258,644

Amount of Gifts-In-Kind $ 1,275,000
Fully Supported USA Personnel Overseas:
Expecting to serve more than 4 years   6
Other Personnel:
Non USA serving in own/other country   3,500
Short-Term less than 1 year from USA   45
Countries: Bangladesh, Bolivia, Brazil, Bulgaria, Cambodia, Central Asia, China, Cuba, Egypt, El Salvador, France, Ghana, Guatemala, India, Indonesia, Ivory Coast, Jordan, Kenya, Korea-S, Laos, Liberia, Macao, Macedonia, Malaysia, Malta, Myanmar, North Africa, Nigeria, Pakistan, Philippines, Senegal, Singapore, South Africa, Sudan, Taiwan, Tanzania, Thailand, Vietnam, Zimbabwe.

◆ ◆ ◆ ◆ ◆

Peter Deyneka Russian Ministries
(630)462-1739   Fax: (630)690-2976
E-Mail: RMUSA@mcimail.com
Web: http://shoga.wwa.com/~strtegy/
P.O. Box 496, Wheaton, IL 60189
Dr. Peter Deyneka, President

An interdenominational support agency of evangelical tradition engaged in Bible and literature distribution, support of national workers, and mission-related research.

"To promote indigenous evangelism and church growth in the former Soviet Union by developing creative and strategic partnerships between nationals and Western Christians."

Year Founded in USA   1991
Income for Overseas Ministries $ 1,545,737
Fully Supported USA Personnel Overseas:
Expecting to serve more than 4 years   2
Expecting to serve 1 up to 4 years   1
Nonresidential mission personnel   7
Other Personnel:
Non USA serving in own/other country   28
Home ministry & office staff in USA   11
Countries: Russia 3.

◆ ◆ ◆ ◆ ◆

Pioneers

(407)382-6000   **Fax: (407)382-1008**
E-Mail: 74511.1250@compuserve.com
Web: http://www.pioneers.org
12343 Narcoossee Rd., Orlando, FL 32827
Rev. John E. Fletcher, Exec. Director
 An interdenominational sending agency of evangelical tradition engaged in church planting, evangelism, discipleship, leadership development, and short-term programs coordination.
 ".. mobilizes teams to glorify God among unreached peoples by initiating church planting movements in partnership with local churches."
Year Founded in USA   1979
Income for Overseas Ministries $ 6,882,572
Fully Supported USA Personnel Overseas:
 Expecting to serve more than 4 years   228
Other Personnel:
 Non USA serving in own/other country   13
 Bi-Vocational/Tentmakers from USA   147
 Short-Term less than 1 year from USA   70
 Home ministry & office staff in USA   25
Countries: Albania 11, Asia-Gen 70, Belize 4, Bolivia 8, Bosnia 5, Croatia 8, Ghana, Guyana 1, Hungary 2, Indonesia 57, Japan 6, Kyrgyzstan 7, Macedonia 2, Mali, N Mariana Isls 1, Nepal 2, Nigeria, Papua New Guin 14, Russia 6, Senegal 6, Thailand 9, Turkey 3, Uzbekistan 4, Zambia 2.

Pocket Testament League

(717)626-1919   **Fax: (717)626-5553**
E-Mail: TPTL@prolog.net
P.O. Box 800, Lititz, PA 17543
Rev. Michael J. McCaskey, Exec. Director
 An interdenominational service agency of evangelical tradition engaged in Scripture distribution, broadcasting, church establishing, evangelism, and training.
 "To assist and equip Christians worldwide in the effective proclamation of the Gospel of Jesus Christ through a coordinated program of Scripture distribution and evangelism."
Year Founded in USA   1908
Income for Overseas Ministries $ 370,722
Fully Supported USA Personnel Overseas:
 Expecting to serve more than 4 years   2

Other Personnel:

Non USA serving in own/other country   150
Home ministry & office staff in USA   12

Countries: Austria 1, Brazil, France, Germany 1, India, Indonesia, Korea-S, Mexico, Philippines, Poland, Portugal, Spain, Thailand, Yugoslavia.

◆ ◆ ◆ ◆ ◆

Prakash Association USA
(408)722-2244   Fax: (408)662-8851
9081 Soquel Dr., Aptos, CA 95003
Mr. Vern Hart, Exec. Director

An interdenominational agency of Baptist tradition supporting national workers, Christian education, and agricultural programs for evangelism, Bible distribution, and church planting.

".. to support the training of nationals to become Christian businessmen and spiritual leaders ... and carry out personal evangelism..."

Year Founded in USA   1969
Income for Overseas Ministries $ 149,919
Fully Supported USA Personnel Overseas:

Nonresidential mission personnel   1

Other Personnel:

Non USA serving in own/other country   35
Home ministry & office staff in USA   1

Countries: India.

◆ ◆ ◆ ◆ ◆

RREACH International
(972)702-0303
E-Mail: RREACHint@aol.com
6350 LBJ Freeway #250, Dallas, TX 75240
Dr. Ramesh Richard, President

A nondenominational support agency of evangelical tradition engaged in leadership development, TV/radio broadcasting, theological education, funds transmission, and training.

".. to reach weaker economies for the Lord Jesus Christ by evangelizing their opinion leaders and strengthening their pastoral leaders."

Year Founded in USA   1987
Income for Overseas Ministries $ 458,000
Personnel:

Nonresidential personnel partially supported   1

Short-Term less than 1 year from USA   2
Home ministry & office staff in USA   7

◆◆◆◆◆

Seed Company, The
(714)969-4697   **Fax: (714)969-4661**
E-Mail: Seed_Co@wycliffe.org
Web: http://www.wycliffe.org/seedco
P.O. Box 2727, Huntington Beach, CA 92647
Roger Garland, Director
   A nondenominational support agency of evangelical tradition engaged in
funds transmission for Bible translation/distribution, literacy work, and
support of national workers. A ministry of Wycliffe Bible Translators.
   ".. to recruit and nurture prayer and financial partners in support of
translation projects which will be managed by national translators or in
which they will play a central role."
Year Founded in USA   1993
Income for Overseas Ministries $ 269,000
Personnel:
   Home ministry & office staff in USA   1

◆◆◆◆◆

VELA Ministries International
(408)232-5663   **Fax: (408)944-0466**
Web: http://www.gospelcom.net/vela/
2302 Zanker Rd., Suite 129, San Jose, CA 95131
Galo Vasquez, President
   An interdenominational support agency of evangelical tradition engaged
in leadership development, funds transmission, support of national workers,
mobilization for mission, mission-related research, and training.
Year Founded in USA   1990
Income for Overseas Ministries $ 200,000
Fully Supported USA Personnel Overseas:
   Expecting to serve more than 4 years   1
   Nonresidential mission personnel   1
Other Personnel:
   Non USA serving in own/other country   9
   Home ministry & office staff in USA   3
Countries: Mexico 1.

◆ ◆ ◆ ◆ ◆

Voice of China and Asia Missionary Society, Inc.
(818)441-0640   **Fax: (818)441-8124**
P.O. Box 15, Pasadena, CA 91102

Dr. Robert B. Hammond, President

An interdenominational sending agency of evangelical and fundamentalist tradition engaged in support of national workers, Christian education, and evangelism.

Year Founded in USA	1946
Income for Overseas Ministries	NR
Fully Supported USA Personnel Overseas:	
Expecting to serve more than 4 years	1
Nonresidential mission personnel	1
Other Personnel:	
Non USA serving in own/other country	200
Home ministry & office staff in USA	7

Countries: Korea-S 1, Taiwan (ROC).

◆ ◆ ◆ ◆ ◆

World Indigenous Missions
(210)629-0863   **Fax: (210)629-0357**
E-Mail: WIMplant@sat.net
P.O. Box 310627, New Braunfels, TX 78131

Mr. Mark R. Balderson, President

A nondenominational sending agency of charismatic tradition engaged in church planting, evangelism, support of national churches, mobilization for mission, and missionary training.

Year Founded in USA	1981
Income for Overseas Ministries	$ 1,051,000
Fully Supported USA Personnel Overseas:	
Expecting to serve more than 4 years	57
Other Personnel:	
Bi-Vocational/Tentmakers from USA	2
Home ministry & office staff in USA	3

Countries: Bolivia 4, Dominican Rep 2, Indonesia 2, Mexico 35, Philippines 6, Puerto Rico 2, Russia 4, Spain 2.

◆ ◆ ◆ ◆ ◆

World-Wide Missions
(909)793-2009   **Fax: (909)793-6880**
P.O. Box 2300, Redlands, CA 92373
Rev. Fred M. Johnson, Exec. Director
    An interdenominational support agency of evangelical tradition engaged
in support of national workers, church planting, childcare/orphanage
programs, Christian education, funds transmission, and medical work.

Year Founded in USA	1950
Income for Overseas Ministries	$ 1,010,543
Amount of Gifts-In-Kind	$ 341,540

Fully Supported USA Personnel Overseas:

Expecting to serve more than 4 years	4
Expecting to serve 1 up to 4 years	2

Other Personnel:

Non USA serving in own/other country	112

Countries: Bolivia, Brazil 2, Congo/Zaire 1, Haiti 2, India, Kenya, Korea-S, Liberia,
Mexico, Nepal 1, Philippines, Turkey.

◆ ◆ ◆ ◆ ◆

Best Reading

Daniel Rickett

In preparation for the consultation, I asked invitees to list the top three books on partnership in mission and the top three articles. The response was not as strong as I had hoped. Nevertheless, I have listed here all books nominated by two or more respondents. While no articles were selected by more than one respondent, those available in missions journals are included in the Further Reading section.

Bush, Luis and Lorry Lutz. *Partnering in Ministry: The Direction of World Evangelism.* Downers Grove: InterVarsity Press, 1990.
A sequel to the ground-breaking book, *The Family Tie,* by Finley and Lutz (1983), this book provides basic information and practical guidelines for sharing resources with indigenous leaders of Christian ministries. An introduction to the biblical basis of partnering is offered along with the "how-to's" of helping national Christian leaders.

Kraakevik, James and Dotsey Welliver, eds. *Partners in the Gospel: The Strategic Role of Partnership in World Evangelization.* Wheaton: Billy Graham Center, Wheaton College, 1992.
A collection of papers and discussions of the "Working Consultation on Partnership in World Mission" convened at the Billy Graham Center in May, 1991. Through articles, case studies, and working group reports, the book provides an overview of partnership in action in various forms: church-to-church, mission-to-mission, and Two-Thirds World partnerships.

Taylor, William D., ed. *Kingdom Partnerships for Synergy in Missions*.
Pasadena: William Carey Library, World Evangelical Fellowship
Missions Commission, 1994.
The papers and reports of the 1992 WEF Missions Commission conference, "Towards Interdependent Partnerships." In
these pages, twenty-two missions leaders from around the
world share candidly about the structural options and cultural challenges of missions partnerships.

Yohannan, K. P. *Revolution in World Missions*. Lake Mary, FL: Creation House, 1986.
An autobiography of K. P. Yohannan's vision and call to
ministry. It is an inspiring account of how Yohannan launched
the ministry of Gospel for Asia and reveals the core of his
vision and driving passion.

Yohannan, K. P. *Why the World Waits*. Lake Mary, FL: Creation House,
1991.
A critique of North American missions and argument for the
support of native missionaries.

Further Reading

Books

Allen, Roland. *Missionary Methods: St. Paul's or Ours?* Grand Rapids: Eerdmans Publishing, 1962.

Bayne, Stephen F. Jr., ed. *Mutual Responsibility and Interdependence in the Body of Christ: With Related Background Documents.* New York: Seabury Press, n.d.

Beaver, R. Pierce, ed. *The Gospel and Frontier Peoples: A Report of a Consultation December 1972.* Pasadena: William Carey Library, 1973.

Bergquist, James A., and P. K. Manickam. *The Crisis of Dependency in Third World Ministries.* Madras: Christian Literature Society, 1974.

Beyerhaus, Peter, and Henry Lefever. *The Responsible Church and the Foreign Mission.* Grand Rapids: Eerdmans Publishing, 1964.

Bosch, David J. *Transforming Mission: Paradigm Shifts in Theology of Mission.* Maryknoll, NY: Orbis Books, 1991.

Buhlmann, Walbert. *The Coming of the Third Church.* Translated by S. J. Woodhall and A. N. Other. Maryknoll: Orbis Books, 1978.

Bush, Luis. *Funding Third World Missions: The Pursuit of True Christian Partnership.* Singapore/Wheaton, IL: World Evangelical Fellowship Missions Commission, 1990.

Bush, Luis, and Lorry Lutz. *Partnering in Ministry: The Direction of World Evangelism.* Downers Grove: InterVarsity Press, 1990.

Costas, Orlando E. *The Church and its Mission: A Shattering Critique from the Third World.* Wheaton: Tyndale House Publishers, 1974.

Finley, Allen, and Lorry Lutz. *The Family Tie.* Nashville: Thomas Nelson Publishers, 1983.

Fraser, David A., ed. *The Church in New Frontiers for Mission.* Monrovia, CA: Missions Advanced Research and Communications Center, 1983.

Fuller, W. Harold. *Mission-Church Dynamics.* Pasadena: William Carey Library, 1980.

Gerber, Vergil, ed. *Missions in Creative Tension. The Green Lake '71 Compendium.* South Pasadena: William Carey Library, 1971.

Hodges, Melvin. *The Indigenous Church and the Missionary.* South Pasadena, CA: William Carey Library, 1978.

Keyes, Lawrence E. *The Last Age of Missions.* Pasadena: William Carey Library, 1983.

Kraakevik, James, and Dotsey Welliver, eds. *Partners in the Gospel: The Strategic Role of Partnership in World Evangelization.* Wheaton: Billy Graham Center, Wheaton College, 1991.

Kraft, Charles H., and Tom N. Wisley, eds. *Readings in Dynamic Indigeneity.* Pasadena: William Carey Library, 1979.

Lausanne Committee for World Evangelization. *Co-operating in World Evangelization.* Lausanne Occasional Papers, no. 24. Wheaton, IL: Lausanne Committee for World Evangelization, 1983.

Nelson, Marlin L. *Readings in Third World Missions: A Collection of Essential Documents.* Pasadena: William Carey Library, 1976.

———. *The How and Why of Third World Missions: An Asian Case Study.* Pasadena: William Carey Library, 1976.

Newbigin, Lesslie. *One Body, One Gospel, One World: The Christian Mission Today.* London: International Missionary Council, 1958.

Otis, George, Jr. *The Last of the Giants.* Tarrytown, NY: Chosen Books, 1991.

Padilla, C. Rene, ed. *The New Face of Evangelicalism.* Downers Grove: InterVarsity Press, 1976.

Pate, Larry. *From Every People: a Handbook of Two-Thirds World Missions.* Monrovia, CA: Missions Advanced Research and Communications Center, 1989.

Peters, George W. *A Biblical Theology of Missions.* Chicago: Moody Press, 1972.

Shenk, Wilbert R., ed. *Mission Focus: Current Issues.* Scottdale, Pennsylvania: Herald Press, 1980.

Wagner, C. Peter, ed. *Church/Mission Tensions Today.* Chicago: Moody Press, 1972.

Wakatama, Pius. *Independence for the Third World Church.* Downers Grove: InterVarsity Press, 1976.

Articles

Adeyemo, Tokunboh. "The African Church and Selfhood." *Perception* 18 (May 1980): 1–10.

"Andean Consultation on Church-Mission Relations." *Boletin Informativo*, Puente 1 (1980):1–3.

Baba, Panya. "We Need to Work Together to Develop Good Relationships." *Evangelical Missions Quarterly* 26, no. 2 (April 1990): 131–133.

Beyerhaus, Peter. "The Three Selves Formula: Is it Built on Biblical Foundations?" *International Review of Missions* 53 (October 1964): 393–407.

Bosch, David J. "Towards True Mutuality: Exchanging the Same Commodities or Supplementing Each Others' Needs?" *Missiology: An International Review* 6, no. 3 (July 1978): 283–296.

Braaten, Carl E. "The Triune God: The Source and Model of Christian Unity and Mission." *Missiology: An International Review* 28, no. 4 (October 1990): 415–427.

Collins, Travis. "Missions and Churches in Partnership for Evangelism: A Study of The Declaration of Ibadan." *Missiology: An International Review* 23, no. 3 (July 1995): 331–339.

Conn, Harvie M. "The Money Barrier Between Sending and Receiving Churches." *Evangelical Missions Quarterly* 14 (October 1978): 231–239.

Corwin, Charles, and Vinay Samuel. "Assistance Programs Require Partnership." *Evangelical Missions Quarterly* 15 (April 1979): 97–101.

Crawford, John R. "Stewardship in Younger Churches: Observations and Caveats From an Africa Perspective." *Missiology: An International Review* 9 (July 1981): 299–310.

Donald, Kenneth G. "What's Wrong with Foreign Money for National Pastors?" *Evangelical Missions Quarterly* 13 (January 1977): 19–25.

Fernando, Ajith. "'Rich' and 'Poor' Nations and the Christian Enterprise: Some Personal Comments." *Missiology: An International Review* 9, no. 3 (July 1981): 287–298.

Flatt, Donald C. "Priorities in Missions—Personnel or Programme?" *International Review of Mission* 59 (October 1970): 461–469.

Hedlund, Roger E. "Cheaper by the Dozen? Indigenous Missionaries vs. Partnership." *Evangelical Missions Quarterly* 26, no. 3 (July 1990): 274–279.

———. "Post Missionary Asia: One Size Doesn't Fit All." *Evangelical Missions Quarterly* 31, no. 1 (January 1995): 78–84.

Keyes, Lawrence E. "Third World Missionaries: More and Better." *Evangelical Missions Quarterly* 18, no. 4 (October 1982): 216–224.

Keyes, Lawrence E., and Larry D. Pate. "Two-Thirds World Missions: The Next 100 Years." *Missiology: An International Review* 21, no. 2 (April 1993): 187–206.

McGavran, Donald A. "East/West Dialogue, West: Yes, But Don't Copy Us." *Church Growth Bulletin* 15 (November 1978): 235–238.

McGavran, Donald A., James Montgomery, and C. Peter Wagner. "Thrashing Old Straw." *Church Growth Bulletin* (1980): 306–311.

———. "Have We Shackled Missions to the National Church?" *Eternity* (December 1982): 21–23.

Pate, Larry D., and Lawrence E. Keyes. "Emerging Missions in a Global Church." *International Bulletin of Missionary Research* 10, no. 4 (October 1986): 156–165.

———. "The Changing Balance in Global Mission." *International Bulletin of Missionary Research* 15, no. 2 (April 1991): 56–61.

Peters, George W. "Mission-Church Relationships," I and II. *Bibliotheca Sacra* 125(499): 205–215, (500): 300–312.

———. "Pauline Patterns of Church-Mission Relationships." *Evangelical Missions Quarterly* 9 (Winter 1973): 111–118.

Samuel, Vinay, and Chris Sugden. "The Two-Thirds World Church and the Multinational Mission Agencies." *Missiology: An International Review* 10, no. 4 (October 1982): 449–454.

———. "Mission Agencies as Multinationals." *International Bulletin of Missionary Research* 17, no. 4 (October, 1983): 152–155.

Sawatsky, Walter. "After the Glasnost Revolution: Soviet Evangelicals and Western Missions." *International Bulletin of Missionary Research* 16, no. 2 (April 1992): 54–60.

Smith, Robert. "The Use of Foreign Financed National Christian Workers." *International Journal of Frontier Missions* 9, no. 2 (April, 1992): 57–63.

Stanley, Rajamani, Roger Hedlund, and J. P. Masih. "The Curses of Money on Missions to India." *Evangelical Missions Quarterly* 22, no. 3 (July 1986): 294–302.

Taylor, William D. "Lessons of Partnership." *Evangelical Missions Quarterly* 31, no. 4 (October 1995): 406–415.